India's Most Legendary Restaurants

India's Most Legendary Restaurants

EDITED BY
RUTH DSOUZA PRABHU

ALEPH BOOK COMPANY
An independent publishing firm
promoted by *Rupa Publications India*

First published in India in 2024
by Aleph Book Company
7/16 Ansari Road, Daryaganj
New Delhi 110 002

This edition copyright © Aleph Book Company 2024
Introduction copyright © Ruth Dsouza Prabhu 2024
Copyright in individual pieces vests with the respective authors.

Picture Credits on p. 169 constitute an extension of the copyright page.

All rights reserved.

The views and opinions expressed in this book are those of the authors and the facts are as reported by them, which have been verified to the extent possible, and the publishers are not in any way liable for the same.

The publisher has used its best endeavours to ensure that URLs for external websites referred to in this book are correct and active at the time of going to press. However, the publisher has no responsibility for the websites and can make no guarantee that a site will remain live or that the content is or will remain appropriate.

No part of this publication may be reproduced, transmitted, or stored in a retrieval system, in any form or by any means, without permission in writing from Aleph Book Company.

ISBN: 978-81-19635-80-1

1 3 5 7 9 10 8 6 4 2

Printed in India.

This book is sold subject to the condition that it shall not, by way of trade or otherwise, be lent, resold, hired out, or otherwise circulated without the publisher's prior consent in any form of binding or cover other than that in which it is published.

CONTENTS

Introduction: Legends Are Made of This   vii
RUTH DSOUZA PRABHU

1. A Paragon of Culinary Excellence   1
   Paragon, Kozhikode (5)
   RUTH DSOUZA PRABHU

2. The Kababs That Have Defined Lucknow for Over a Century   23
   Tunday Kababi, Lucknow (6)
   ANUBHUTI KRISHNA

3. Nostalgia and the Making of a Legend   47
   Peter Cat, Kolkata (10)
   PRIYADARSHINI CHATTERJEE

4. The Dhaba That Birthed a Town   71
   Amrik Sukhdev Dhaba, Murthal (16)
   OM ROUTRAY

5. A Family's Commitment to Consistency   93
   Mavalli Tiffin Rooms (MTR), Bengaluru (32)
   RUTH DSOUZA PRABHU

6. A Cuisine, a Century, a Legend 117
   Karim's, New Delhi (84)
   OM ROUTRAY

7. Looking to the Future, Staying True 139
   to the Past
   Ram Ashraya, Mumbai (111)
   AATISH NATH

References 163

Picture Credits 169

Notes on the Contributors 170

INTRODUCTION
LEGENDS ARE MADE OF THIS

In June 2023, when Taste Atlas released its list of 150 legendary restaurants of the world, seven Indian establishments featured on it. These were Paragon in Kozhikode (11), Tunday Kababi in Lucknow (12), Peter Cat in Kolkata (17), Amrik Sukhdev Dhaba in Murthal (23), Mavalli Tiffin Rooms (MTR) in Bengaluru (39), Karim's in Delhi (87), and Ram Ashraya in Mumbai (112).* I was approached to work on this book just as I had completed an interview with Sumesh Govind of Paragon for a national publication. Telling the Paragon story was a feature I enjoyed writing, and so the idea of collaborating with writers to tell the stories of the other restaurants on the list was nothing short of exciting.

As I began working on the book with Anubhuti

---

*In December 2023, Taste Atlas released revised rankings: Paragon (5), Tunday Kababi (6), Peter Cat (10), Amrik Sukhdev Dhaba (16), Mavalli Tiffin Rooms (32), Karim's (84), and Ram Ashraya (111). See www.tasteatlas.com/iconic-dishes-legendary-restaurants.

Krishna, Priyadarshini Chatterjee, Om Routray, and Aatish Nath, wonderful writers (and most of them good friends too), the idea was to tell our readers the story of how these legendary restaurants came to be. For those in the world of food, these names are familiar, but their stories are known piecemeal at best.

The question that arose for me was: what makes a restaurant legendary? Is it the food and the recipes that have been handed down over generations? Is it the commitment of the people who built it and the subsequent generations who continued to nurture it? Or maybe it was how these seven restaurants became so intrinsically woven into the fabric of the society they were located within that made them legendary?

To do justice to their stories, we decided that a personalized approach was best. Each writer has had a long-standing equation with the city and the restaurant, which helped craft their narrative. It has been integral to the flow of these essays which are peppered with previously unexplored anecdotes about these much talked about places.

For example, the masala dosas at MTR are among the dishes that are its claim to legendary fame. During the Emergency, when Harishchandra Maiya was forced to lower the price of the dosa, he made sure he did not compromise on its quality. Losses mounted every day, and the restaurant displayed these figures on a board outside.

The kababs at Tunday Kababi are its soul, but did you know that close to 160 spices go into their making? (No, we don't tell you which ones.) Peter Cat was first going to be named Omar Khayyam, and while there is no cat to whom the name can be attributed, there is a serendipitous story to its christening. The story of Amrik Sukhdev Dhaba has it all—family politics, multiple moves, a demolition, and a fire. But what remained constant was that they never stopped serving food through it all. An appam for dinner at Paragon may be de rigueur today, but when Sumesh wanted to introduce it in the menu, the opposition he met with from his team was stupendous. We are happy he prevailed. And then there is Karim's, whose story runs parallel to the development of Delhi as India's capital city. Karim's grew from a cart outside Jama Masjid, eventually finding a spot in Gali Kababiyan in purani Dilli, while all around it, the city was growing into the metropolis we see today.

As I read each essay, I felt I was being transported back in time and reliving the memories and stories as they unfolded. What is true with all of them is the unwavering conviction that each creator had in what they had to offer. There is also the rock-solid commitment to providing diners with a culinary experience that has remained unchanged over time. Yes, the restaurants have grown, even modernized a little in some cases, but the food, the flavours, and the nostalgia packed into every bite is a joy that families and friends have savoured through the generations.

What perhaps adds to the creation of the legendary status of these places, besides the grit and passion with which they have been nurtured, is their continuing humility, how they offer everyday fare that people relish. They may not be Michelin-starred, but the service remains from the heart and the food is unrivalled in quality.

This is an easy book to read. I urge you to settle in with a cup of tea and possibly a snack because the food you will read about will make you hungry. Choose to read in sequence—the essays are ordered according to the restaurant's place in the Taste Atlas list—or dip into any essay you like. If you are familiar with the food and the restaurant, you will now have fresh context and something new to talk about on your next visit. If you haven't visited the restaurant yet, these stories will ensure you add it to your must-eat-at list, if it doesn't already feature there.

We hope you enjoy this book as much as we enjoyed eating our way through our interviews and research at these restaurants.

Ruth Dsouza Prabhu

A PARAGON OF CULINARY EXCELLENCE

Paragon, Kozhikode (5)

Ruth Dsouza Prabhu

Paragon's facade at its flagship outlet in Kozhikode is hard to miss. One half is exposed brick, and the other half is a white canopied entryway into the restaurant. The well-known red and white logo on the brick wall reminds patrons that the restaurant has been functional since 1939. And placed high above, looking all the more imposing at night when it is lit up, is the name of the restaurant in bold capitals.

There is always a line outside Paragon—families, groups of friends, and even a few solo diners amongst them all. No matter the heat, humidity, or even the rain, everyone patiently waits their turn to be called inside and seated. The promise of a great meal is one that the restaurant has steadfastly kept—generations of diners will vouch for this.

Over the years, Paragon has grown. Driven by innovation, they have established branches in Kochi, Trivandrum, Dubai, and Bengaluru (this last being its newest and the first one outside of Kerala, but within India). Additionally, Sumesh Govind, managing director of the Paragon Group of Restaurants, has launched other restaurants like MGrill which serves Italian, French, and Thai cuisine; Salkara which specializes in Malabari food; Brown Town, the brand's European bakery and cafe with some Asian influences, and Paragon's catering division. Together, these ventures provide employment opportunities for approximately 3,000 people spread across thirty-six outlets.

I met Sumesh over lunch one day. He strode in, wearing a simple black tee and jeans, and with an energy belying his fifty-nine years. Instantly, everyone in the restaurant perked up, many with broad smiles seeing the boss walk in. I soon realized that what I initially mistook for deference for Sumesh's position was respect for a man who has carried the legacy of Paragon firmly on his shoulders since 1988–89. 2023 marked eighty-four years since Paragon first opened its doors in Kozhikode. Sumesh took me back in time to when it all began.

Rewind Eighty-four Years

The year was 1939. Govindan Panchikail, Sumesh's paternal grandfather, had retired from the Indian Railways. With time on his hands to now follow his culinary passions, he opened a bakery in Kozhikode with his son, P. M. Valsan, christening it Paragon. The story goes that a high-ranking British official and his wife were good friends with Govindan. It was this official's wife who suggested the name Paragon Baking Company—perhaps foreseeing the legacy that could be built.

The bakery became the go-to place for Kozhikode residents looking for flaky puffs, indulgent Christmas cakes, and other baked goods. 'People would come from as far as Trivandrum and Kochi to buy from us. We also had a small restaurant attached to the bakery which served a few signature dishes like mutton chops curry paired with bread and Kerala's famous combination of appam with vegetable or mutton stew,' reminisces Sumesh.

Sumesh's memories of his grandfather are faint, but he tells me that his father took charge of Paragon soon after Govindan's passing. 'The restaurant did well with my father at the helm, and he chose to expand into other businesses. He married my mother, Saraswati Valsan, and I was born in 1963,' he says. However, the diversification did not go as planned and Valsan incurred huge losses which immensely affected his morale.

Sumesh's family ploughed on, surviving the best they could despite the financial pressures they were under. He believes that the strain took a toll on his father who passed away in 1978, when Sumesh was only fifteen years old. Despite her grief, Saraswati, Sumesh's mother, was sure that she wanted to carry Paragon's legacy forward. No small task, considering small-town Kozhikode (like most other places) back then was quite averse to having women at the forefront of a business. The pride and respect for what his mother lived through and achieved during those tough years is evident as Sumesh tells me of those times.

'You have to remember that Paragon was not a fine-dining restaurant, but a typical Malayali one, and my mother must have been among the first ladies in Kozhikode to take over such a business.' Saraswati would sit at the cash counter and supervise every aspect of the restaurant's workings. She carried on relentlessly despite the disapprobation of society and even members of the family being unhappy about it.

As for Sumesh, he was at that time a typical teenager, no longer kept in check by a strict father. 'I had the time of my life,' he says. 'Rather than helping out, I was part of the problem for my mother.' Saraswati was battling several issues—the loss of her husband, the growing pains of a teenager, running a restaurant with the everyday rigmarole of staff issues, customer complaints, and more. She was also tackling the burden of debt and dealing with a judgemental society. At one point, she was faced with eviction when a large part of the Paragon building was acquired by the government for building a flyover. The staff who had been with the business for close to forty years went on strike against the acquisition, posing significant hurdles for the restaurant. Their protest continued until a solution was arrived at.

'My mother was constantly between the devil and the deep blue sea, but she handled it all well,' Sumesh says with respect and admiration.

A teenager during those turbulent years, Sumesh saw only chaos and didn't want to have anything to do with the restaurant. When he completed his commerce degree, he stated emphatically that Paragon was not his cup of tea. 'Like most youngsters, I believed I was a genius at philosophy, literature, art, movie critiquing—all subjects I was interested in and completely into,' he chuckled.

But there came a time when the family was up against the wall. The debts continued to linger, and the restaurant's prospects had grown stagnant. The question arose: should Sumesh sell the restaurant and use that money to follow his passion or should he step in and try to fix things? To find the answer, he turned to his spiritual guru.

'It is in your karma that you have to get into the family business. Do what is in your hands right now, and then work on becoming what you like later,' his guru had guided Sumesh. 'This advice made sense to me. Here I was, not doing what was in front of me and what was needed of me, instead wanting to go into literature and the like. I understood that I needed to walk the talk before I do anything else, and so I decided to take matters into my own hands.' And that's what Sumesh did around 1988–89.

An Era of Innovation

The first thing the restaurant needed was an infusion of money to get it back on its feet. This came to Sumesh from a well-wisher and family friend named Girija. It helped bring the business back on track and keep it steadily moving forward. With that done, Sumesh began to bring in what he knew would truly turn the tide for Paragon—

innovation. He did this with the food and, a first for its time and the place, with human resources initiatives. Hiring processes were restructured with a focus on recruiting qualified members for the team, employee welfare measures were put in place, and staff quarters introduced. In six months, Paragon was back to its earlier glory.

Sumesh elaborates upon his approach to the business: 'I strongly felt that innovation and creativity would transform what I perceived as monotonous operations. But with time, I also realized that being creative cannot be in isolation and has to be done in totality. While being creative was important, being disruptive with it was equally necessary. With this realization, I put all my philosophical knowledge into practice, and I started slowly introducing change.'

The quality of the food was where he placed the spotlight to begin with.

Restaurants, especially those with a long legacy, have one or two dishes that they are best known for. In Bengaluru, Vidyarthi Bhavan's dosas, the raspberry soda at Britannia & Co. in Mumbai, and the shami kabab at Wenger's in New Delhi are what people return for time and again. But with Paragon, Sumesh points out, they have as many as twenty specialties. 'We don't rely on just one or two dishes but a whole array of them. We began an R&D section for the kitchen, brought in new chefs, and began working on new ideas.'

At this point in our conversation, we were well into lunchtime and Sumesh gave me the chance to taste several specialties. We started with the chef's signature shrimp—marinated tiger prawns that are pan sautéed with plenty of flavourful garlic, slit green chillies, and a touch of coconut cream. He watched me closely as I picked up a prawn by the tail and took that first bite, waiting to see what I thought of his first recommendation. The light, crunchy exterior was like perfectly done tempura, but with all the goodness of a moderately spicy masala. The hot prawns were soft on the inside, not chewy, and when eaten with some of the fried garlic and chillies, made for a perfect starter to the meal. Once I finished the plate of prawns, I found myself constantly reaching out to pick up the delicious crumbs on the plate.

Next up was a fish mango curry. Coming from Mangaluru, where fish curries for lunch are a staple, I can say that this is one curry I would gladly eat every day of the week. The gravy is silky because of the coconut milk and the tartness of the mango slices through, whether you mop it up with a flaky Kerala parotta or some hot steamed rice, both of which I did. The kozhi porichathu or the Malabari style chicken 65—deep-fried chunks of marinated chicken—is a dish that I wished came in a family-size bucket.

'When we worked on our dishes, we aimed for perfection, but to achieve that, you need innovation. When you are trying to recreate a classic dish, nobody is going to part with their secret to making it the perfect one. You have to tread your own path and keep remaking the dish till you achieve the classic taste you are looking for.' And that is what Sumesh and his team of chefs did.

Perfecting a classic was one area of focus when it came to innovation; the other was coming up with something new that would excite diners. 'When a customer walks in, there are two things he asks for—what are the classics and what's new,' explains Sumesh. But new was not always easy to achieve.

It was Sumesh's friend, Shakil Ahmed, who reminded him of something from their youth. 'He asked me if I recalled how I ate ayla (mackerel), and I remembered how I used to enjoy having a whole mackerel at one go. I would ask my mother not to cut it up but instead serve it whole with onion and tomato slices. It paired perfectly with a peg of Old Monk rum,' he laughs. And so a fond food memory turned into an innovative experiment and went on to become an iconic dish at Paragon.

Sumesh told his team that they would introduce a whole mackerel on a big plate, served in fine dining style with accompaniments, and would charge ₹30–35 (this was about thirty years ago) for it. 'They [the team] were sure that no one would be willing to shell out more than ₹10 in those days for a mackerel, whole or half, let alone almost triple the price. But I stuck to my guns and insisted on bringing this into the menu. The staff asked me to arm them with helmets that would protect them against the blows they were sure the diners would rain on them. I told them to simply direct anyone looking to throw a punch in my direction, and we went live with the idea,' he says.

Just a few days after the introduction of the whole mackerel, Sumesh found that almost every table at the restaurant had ordered the dish: 'People were so happy that someone had thought of something like this and that someone in this little town was finally going the gourmet way.'

A second innovation for food lovers came about from another childhood memory and was met with equal, if not more resistance, by the staff at Paragon.

Appam is a breakfast staple usually served with mutta (egg) curry. It is not typically made for other meals. However, Sumesh's mother would often prepare it for dinner—hot appams served with kunji matthi (small sardine) stir fry and leftover gravy from lunch. 'It was sheer heaven for us as a meal, and I thought why not start serving appam at night? It was something no one had done in Kerala yet.'

The opposition Sumesh faced from his team was incredible—for once they took a united stand. Their argument against introducing appams for dinner was that the restaurant had a fixed turnover every night with people coming in to enjoy their share of Kerala parotta and chilli or ginger chicken. But if Paragon was to serve appam at night, people would ask for kadala curry (black channa in a coconut gravy) to go with it and the billing of ₹100 would come down to ₹30–40, leading to a dip in sales. The appam idea was stalled.

However, Sumesh was convinced that it would work and gave the team a deadline to implement the idea. What was first needed was for the appam kadais (a round deep-frying pan designed specifically for appams to have a thick fluffy centre and lacy edges) to be installed. But the staff continued to delay the process, saying the masons did not turn up for work. Finally, Sumesh had had enough. He fetched the mason and supervised the work himself. He got the laterite stands and kadais with in-built burners set up, and the appam made an appearance on the menu. This proved to be a turning point for the restaurant, and sales skyrocketed within a few days. 'People wanted appam with everything, and even today it is one of our biggest hits.'

'The thing about Paragon was that back in the day in Kozhikode, this was *the* only place for a meal outside,' says Saina Jayapal, a public relations consultant currently based in Bengaluru. If you were celebrating something, you went to the air-conditioned section of the restaurant. For everyday meals, it was the non-air-conditioned section or takeaway. For me, as a child brought up in the Gulf and returning to a sleepy town like Kozhikode in the early 90s, Paragon was my respite.'

Saina has dined at the Bengaluru outlet too. She remains loyal and partial to the Kozhikode branch but agrees that Sumesh has managed to make the restaurant work well in a new city because his focus on consistency remains unwavering. For her, on every visit home, whether it was during her hostel days in Mangaluru and Manipal in the early 2000s or now as a professional in Bengaluru, a meal at Paragon is a must.

'My favourite dishes include the prawn dry fry, prawn mango curry, the chicken biryani, and parottas. I also never miss having the masala fried chicken. But what I love the most are the regular meals served here. I may order a fish dish to go with it, but the plate is made up of a variety of quintessential Kerala dishes—spinach or cheera (red amaranth) thoran, rasam, chammanthi (dry spicy coconut chutney), payasam, and papadam along with boiled rice. It is so homely. And the dancing tea is always a delight,' she says. Dancing tea is a hot tea set in layers of sugar syrup, steeped black tea, and frothy milk such that the layers appear to be dancing in the tall glass as it is brought to the table. One can sip it slowly and watch the layers blend into each other, or simply stir it all together and drink it. A similar version is the KT chai or Kalladka chai at Hotel Laxmi Nivas on the outskirts of Mangaluru.

Whenever Saina's family in Kozhikode wants to order biryani, it is always from Paragon. And interestingly, she points out how in a state that is partial to its beef biryanis, it is the chicken version that Paragon is famous for.

The chicken biryani is a dish that Sumesh has worked on for almost eight years along with Chef Vijayan Pillai, Paragon's biryani masterchef. Together they travelled and sampled biryanis from several places. Ustads, best described as cooks at small, generations-old eateries who staunchly resist change despite having built their legacy by giving a traditional dish their own twist, were brought into the restaurant. This gave the chefs at Paragon a chance to observe them at work, imbibe what they were willing to share, and all this went into creating Paragon's legendary biryani.

Paragon uses what they refer to as leg-on chicken, which gives the robust flavour of country chicken. The rice (the jeerakasala variety also known as kaima) and meat are cooked separately, with ghee, onions, ginger, garlic, tomatoes, coriander, and fried onions going in at different stages, along with a biryani masala created by Chef Vijayan, giving the dish a unique Paragon touch. Today, they sell between 500 and 700 kilograms of biryani a day at the Kozhikode outlet. They also have versions of the dish with mutton, prawn, fish, and vegetables.

'The beautiful thing about Paragon has been that we have the entire gamut of customers coming in. We have regulars who are die-hard fans of our biryani and chicken dry fry. There are also senior citizens who enjoy a meal with us. I have seen newly married couples come, then later bringing their children, who are now married and visiting us with their young ones. Hopefully, I will also be able to see another generation of regular customers,' Sumesh wishes.

While the legacy that Paragon has built for itself has given it a loyal diner base, it has also put the restaurant on the must-visit list of those passing through the city.

The list of celebrities from the corporate and film world and top politicians that have visited Paragon also runs long, from singer Usha Uthup to actor and director M. Nassar, writer Chetan Bhagat, actors R. Madhavan and Abhishek Bachchan, filmmaker Mira Nair, and politician Nitin Gadkari. Soon after the Taste Atlas announcement, actress Sunny Leone visited the outlet. She mentioned in a video on the restaurant's social media page that this was the first restaurant she was visiting in Kerala in eleven years. Emirati YouTuber, vlogger, and digital content creator Khalid Al Ameri flew over 2,000 kilometres from Dubai to Kozhikode to try the biryani and was left speechless. And this is just in Kozhikode. Even their outlet in Dubai sees a steady stream of Indian and international glitterati.

If there is one thing that echoes across all social media posts, it's that the consistency of Paragon's food has remained steady as a rock over the years. This is possible only when staff at the restaurant are as invested in its success as the owners. Right from the time Sumesh took over the restaurant and its operations, he knew that the people who work for him are its beating heart and that only if he looked after them would they reciprocate the love.

Investing in People

Once things started looking up after he took over, Sumesh realized that he was making a difference in the lives of several underprivileged people in society.

'People come into the restaurant business when they have no other option. You don't need any qualifications to clean a table or serve food. For many, it was the last resort, and I wanted to do the best possible for them because I knew it would make them more efficient at their work. There is, of course, the business I was running, but in a way, it was also an act of altruism. My staff was well taken care of; I was fair to them, offered better wages, and encouraged good team spirit. Rather than commanding them, I approached them with a sense of comradeship and ensured that they were there to guide each other.'

Leading the way for best practices in the restaurant business, Sumesh was the first in Kerala to provide staff quarters to his employees. It comprised rooms for four with an attached bathroom. A watchman was hired for security. He also brought in a human resources professional. A chartered accountant handled finances. Executive chefs, a corporate chef from a reputed five-star hotel, and experienced managers were recruited.

Every accolade that Paragon has received has been celebrated with the entire team. Sumesh also discovered that his staff appreciated working with him because he had a street-smart approach and a knack for knowing what would work. 'I knew that to grow and help them grow as well, I had to create more opportunities, and hence the expansion plan.'

Sumesh believes in creating the finest version of each dish they serve: 'In Dubai, I have Café Calicut alongside Calicut Paragon where I serve the best Wagyu beef burgers and pastas. At Brown Town in Kozhikode, people love our continental dishes. At MGrill we have as many as five to six cuisines. The Bengaluru outlet of Paragon too has a mix of cuisines, though the focus is on Malabar food. But, I insist that if we are offering a dish from any cuisine, it has to be the best or we don't do it at all.'

This fact was validated twice for me—once when I visited Paragon in Bengaluru with my family and saw the likes of cream of tomato soup, Arabian mezze platter, Caesar salad, and Hakka noodles being ordered as much as their biryani, nool parotta, and lemon tea. The second time Sumesh's words rang true was when I saw a social media post of a massive order at Paragon which included a paneer dish. A few of the commenters on the post raised an eyebrow, only to be silenced by the poster who said that it was the softest paneer they had ever eaten.

'I dabble in multiple cuisines because when it comes to food, I can't think of borders. One day I find myself yearning for a good biryani, and another day a pasta. We can be adventurous with food, and I wanted to say that with my restaurants,' says Sumesh.

Over time, Sumesh has found that the only way forward for him has been to constantly challenge himself and not stay in a comfort zone. 'Such challenges help me stay young. I believe that the restaurant business is not rocket science; anyone with the right attitude and common sense can do it. For me, to be able to employ people from across society is satisfying and a huge motivating factor. Most of my team members have been with me for years now and are getting younger with me,' he chuckles. Chef Vijayan has been with Paragon for over thirty years now. Chartered accountant A. Unnikrishnan Menon was first hired to handle finances when Sumesh took control of the business. Today he is the chief operations officer of the company. Chef Thomas has been with Paragon for fifteen years and is their corporate chef. There are several such folks at the Paragon Group of Restaurants.

At this point in the story, Sumesh tells me he must

mention the role his wife, Liju Govind, has played in the success of the restaurants. 'It is because of her support, the way she cares for my family and my mother that I can do all that I have achieved today. She is the person I am eternally indebted to.'

A month or so after the opening of the Bengaluru branch, once the long waiting lines had subdued a bit, our family headed there for lunch. There was still a waiting list, but from the earlier hour-long time frames, it was down to twenty minutes, probably due to the festive holiday during which we chose to make this plan. As promised, we were ushered to a table that was being cleaned and set up as we were approaching it.

Once seated, menus in hand, we took our time to browse through, even though for the most part we knew what we wanted. The first dish to come to the table was the chef's special prawns and the fish mango curry which I was so sure of after dining with Sumesh. We paired that with some nool parotta, and I was so happy to see that my family enjoyed it just as much as I first did. And not to let go of that wonderful curry served in a clay chatti (a wide-mouthed clay pot), we ordered some boiled rice to go with it.

A plate of chemeen porichathu—steaming masala-soaked prawns—was next. The well-cooked prawns were spicy enough that we were grateful for the pacha maanga (raw mango) drink and the grape nannari sharbath which we had ordered. Appams followed, to be enjoyed with both the fish curry and the prawns. And then we asked for the chicken biryani. Unfortunately, it had run out by 2 p.m. Disappointed as we were, I thought this meant that I had to try my luck on another visit. We asked for the caramel custard and elaneer payasam and then wrapped up our meal with the dancing tea and lemon tea.

Sitting back with our teas, I watched a restaurant brimming to capacity—tables filled up as soon as they were cleared. But the staff did not seem harried nor did I hear any table complain about a delay. As food was being served, several takeaway parcels were being prepped at the open kitchen counters. When we were getting ready to pay the bill, we saw pans of steaming biryani coming out of the kitchen and jumped to place a takeaway order. I was going to get to sample that biryani after all.

I came away from the restaurant seeing how well Sumesh's holistic approach to innovating on the ground at Paragon has borne fruit. According to him, he has long since understood that much more than telling stories, he was creating one, and it was a tough task: 'I always ask: how can we better ourselves?'

Over a span of more than eight decades, Paragon in Kozhikode has firmly etched its mark in the hearts and palates of countless patrons. Sumesh Govind, through his dedication and vision, has masterfully woven the restaurant's story, turning it into a gastronomic haven that stands as a testament to the power of tradition, innovation, and unwavering excellence. Paragon's evolution epitomizes the art of creating timeless experiences, through flavours that linger and stories that endure.

Must-have Dishes at Paragon

Chicken biryani

The biryani is among the many highlights at Paragon. Tightly packed into the serving dish, it comes to the table steaming hot, inviting you to dig in right away. As you serve the rice onto your plate, its light hues of yellow give way to a more robust green-brown of the masala-coated meat. The aromatics take over at this point, and you partake of your first bite even as you blow on your fingers to soothe the heat. The ghee is evident and is a perfect foil to the robust flavours of the masala, all coming together for a satisfying mouthful. Served with chammanthi (a spicy dry coconut chutney), pickle, and papadam, this dish is happiness guaranteed.

Fish or prawn mango curry

It is said you feast with your eyes first, and this velvety curry served in the wide-mouthed clay chatti will tempt you to dip a finger in right away. Generous with the number of large prawns in it, the combination of the nuttiness of coconut, the spice from the red chilli, and the tartness of raw mango chunks make this a perfect combination with boiled rice, appam, or even puttu. Squash the raw mango into the curry to elevate the experience.

Chef's special prawns

At first glance, it's the crunchy, brown, fresh-off-the-pan glisten on the prawns that catches your eye. The crispy first bite gives way to juicy prawns that have subtly taken to the marinade. These are served with the tail on, and not for a minute should you hesitate to squeeze out all the meat ensconced inside.

Vegetarian meals

Sometimes, nothing satisfies the soul more than a simple vegetarian meal and the one at Paragon delivers and how. The beauty of this meal is that it is always a delectable spread of seasonal vegetables made in many ways, just like you would at home. What remains standard is the Kerala-style sambar, curd, pickle, chammanthi, papadam, and payasam.

Dancing tea

This is tea served in a tall glass and works with the power of density to create a visual delight. It begins with a decoction of dark tea, topped with a layer of milk, which when shaken as it comes to your table begins to swirl into tea. This is finished off with a tall layer of frothy peaks of milk. Stir the liquid to bring it together, or sip directly into it and let gravity do the mixing for you!

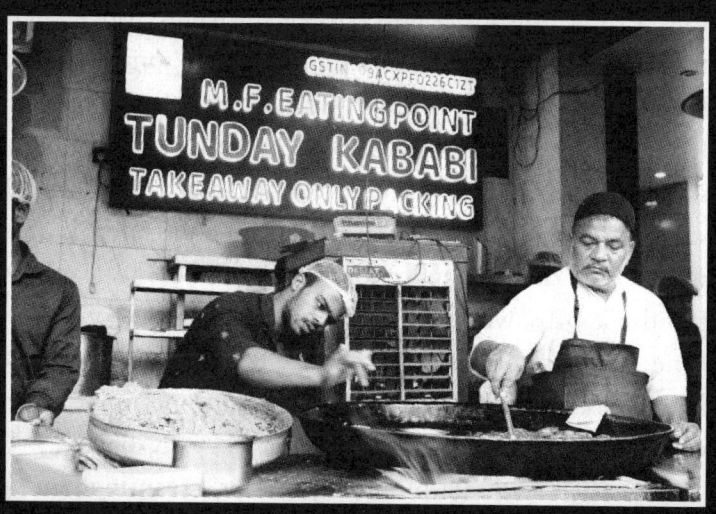

THE KABABS THAT HAVE DEFINED LUCKNOW FOR OVER A CENTURY

Tunday Kababi, Lucknow (6)

Anubhuti Krishna

At noon on a hot summer day, the fires are already blazing at Tunday Kababi in Lucknow's Aminabad. On one stove sits an inverted karahi with clouds of smoke billowing from it. The young man standing behind the stove rolls a large ball of dough between his palms, pats it onto the karahi, presses it with a cloth, applies some oil, and flips it until it cooks on both sides. In less than a minute, he turns out four parathas. Behind him on a platform, stands an army of men who work in an assembly line of sorts. Two men make small kababs from a pre-mixed meat mince and drop them onto a large griddle, two others flip the kababs, while a third pours molten ghee on them. One person's sole responsibility is to pick up the ready kababs and either serve them on a white melamine plate or place them in a small cardboard takeaway box.

Nearby, two aluminium pots sit steaming on a stainless steel stand, the sweet scent of screw pine and cardamom from them filling the air. A man next to these pots dishes out plate after plate of saffron-hued rice with succulent pieces of meat and hands the biryani over to the servers. Every few minutes, two others replace the empty pot with a freshly filled one. And in front of all these men who are working, without even looking up from their griddles, karahis, or degs for hours on end, are over two dozen customers—either waiting for their orders to be packed or for a seat inside the massive two-storeyed restaurant that is always full.

I've been coming to Tunday Kababi for twenty-five years and nothing seems to have changed over these years. If anything, the number of people waiting in line has grown, as has the amount of biryani being served, and the kababs are now made non-stop through the day. From a small one-storey place, the restaurant has become a multi-storeyed outlet with a capacity of more than 400, and yet there is never enough space for those who want to eat their legendary kabab. The kababs are never in short supply though—whether you come at noon or midnight, you will always find kababs and biryani ready, even if you cannot find a place to sit.

A Walk Back in Time

The story of Lucknow's Tunday Kababi is oft-repeated in food circuits and among regular diners as well. The popular lore talks of a gifted one-handed kababchi (master of the grilled kabab), Haji Murad Ali (aka Tunday mian; Tunday meaning one-hand; mian is an Urdu title of respect), creating melt-in-mouth kababs for a king who had lost his teeth but not his will to eat. This story, however, is not completely accurate. But before we dive into the real story of Tunday Kababi and what makes it so iconic, a little history of Lucknow and the evolution of its cuisine, of which the galawat ke kabab is an intrinsic part, is in order.

'To understand the story of galawat ke kabab—not galawati kabab as people tend to call them, but kabab made with galawat, the tenderizer (papaya in this case), that gives them the name—one needs to go back in history to understand why the kababs of Lucknow are so delicate and different from their counterparts across India,' journalist Mehru Jaffer, who is from Lucknow and has worked extensively on the region's history, tells me when I talk to her about Tunday Kababi. Jaffer goes on to outline the complex yet little-known history of the nawabs of Awadh, the region that lies around the present-day cities of Ayodhya, Lucknow, and Kanpur. The nawabs were connoisseurs of fine food and patrons of high culture. Of Persian descent, they had inherited the great taste of their forefathers, and it was under their reign that Awadh became the centre of arts, crafts, music, poetry, and architecture and was often compared to Persia and Byzantium.

'Following the Treaty of Allahabad in 1765, when the nawab of Awadh, Shuja-ud-Daula, was no longer allowed to have an army, he built himself a palace in Faizabad. With ample wealth and time on hand, the nawabs, who possessed pedigree, began patronizing arts and culture in the kingdom,' explains Jaffer. With time, Shuja-ud-Daula's son, Asaf-ud-Daula, known as the 'Architect of Lucknow', moved the capital of Awadh from Faizabad to Lucknow. This town, which was once just a dusty granary of the Mughals, was transformed into a cultural paradise. This rise of the nawabs of Awadh and the city of Lucknow coincided with the fall of the Mughals and the decline of Delhi. And so, some of the finest dancers, singers, poets, and cooks of Delhi, who suddenly found themselves without a patron, migrated to Lucknow. This further cemented the city's place in the cultural landscape of India. It was then, sometime in the eighteenth century, that the cuisine of Awadh reached its zenith.

To impress their patrons, the khansamas, bawarchis, and rasoiyas (khansamas, informs Jaffer, were the head of the kitchen and supervised everything; the bawarchis and rasoiyas were line chefs who did most of the cooking) innovated dishes that challenged their skills and knowledge. The food served at the homes of nobility became a symbol of their wealth and determined their position in society. According to word on the street, the unique dishes that were cooked in Lucknow during the late eighteenth century included exquisite creations like the motia pulav (a preparation of the finest rice and meat shaped into small balls and coloured with egg-white so they glimmered like real pearls), goat mussalam (an entire goat was stuffed with chicken, which in turn was stuffed with a quail, and the quail with minced meat and egg, after which the whole thing was roasted on an open fire till it was cooked through), and various types of qormas, kalias, and kababs that had the most complex recipes, unique spice blends, and delicate flavours.

While the nawabs and their wealth are long gone, these flavours have prevailed. Galawat ke kabab is just one of the many examples of the culinary heritage that Lucknow has held onto. Made with fine mincemeat (originally buffalo, but now also mutton), the kabab is known for its unique texture, thanks to the galawat that turns the meat almost pâté-like. Tunday Kababi has been the flag bearer of this culinary legacy for over 118 years.

'There are three things that make Tunday so special: the first, of course, is the lore of Tunday mian, the second is the spice blend he is said to have created in consultation with Hakim Safdar Nawab, one of the most popular hakims in the early 1900s, and the third, and most important, that this was the food of the common man,' explains Professor Pushpesh Pant, noted author, historian, and academician, known for his in-depth knowledge of regional Indian cuisines and the Indian foodscape. Professor Pant has not only seen the establishment grow from a humble shack to the empire it is today, but he has also known the family for decades. 'I have had the good fortune of eating kababs made by Tunday mian's nephew Haji Rais Ahmad, who was a great kababchi and a noble man,' he remembers, adding that Rais inherited not just the recipes but also the talent from his uncle. He took over the business after Tunday mian's passing, and the establishment is now run by his son, Mohammad Usman.

Many dismiss Tunday ke kabab as cheap street food that lacks the refinement of kababs that are prepared in the homes of Lucknow's elite families. However, Professor Pant believes the kababs at Tunday Kababi are exceptional. In his opinion, it is not just the quality of ingredients and the blend of the masalas (which no one else in Lucknow has been able to master) that makes it special, but it is also the technique of frying involved: 'The whole process of frying it in a brass lagan (a large flat vessel), on imli ka koyla (tamarind wood charcoal) where you keep moving the vessel to regulate heat, also plays a role in making the kababs so wonderfully textured. Then of course, the experience of queuing with dozens of others, getting your kababs on a pattal (leaf plate), and eating them with a paratha adds to the charm.'

As someone who grew up a vegetarian in Lucknow, my introduction to meat happened sometime in 2002 with the delicious buffalo meat kabab at Tunday Kababi. Its meatiness did play on my mind, but one bite of the soft kabab made me a convert. Decades later, and after eating some of the finest food in the world, the kabab here remains one of my favourite things to eat and is the only place in the city where I eat galawat ke kabab. I am not alone; I know hundreds who eat kababs only at Tunday even if means they have to wait months, sometimes years to visit.

'Around twenty-five years ago, when I first started coming to Tunday, I was a young man with hardly any money, and yet I visited Lucknow just to eat at Tunday,' shares Debashish Kar, who lives and works out of Gurugram. 'As young men, my friends and I would eat half a dozen kababs at one go and then pack another dozen. Before it moved to its current location in Aminabad, we visited the original Tunday outlet in Chowk a few kilometres away. We now come to Aminabad because it is more accessible, friendlier, has better seating, and is cleaner,' he says. Over the years, Debashish has returned to Tunday Kababi regularly with family, friends, and even strangers. 'The food here is outstanding. The buffalo kabab is the finest you will ever eat. I also love the mutton qorma, which I feel is so layered that it takes a few visits for you to decipher its flavours,' he tells me, adding that he doesn't eat these two things anywhere else in the world, even in Lucknow.

The People Who Built the Legacy

Now on to the story of the one-handed kababchi. Haji Murad Ali was a gifted kababchi who arrived in Lucknow from Bhopal in search of work. As luck would have it, one evening he fell off a rooftop while flying a kite. His arm was badly injured, and in the absence of proper medical care, he lived with the festering wound for a long time.

One day, he met a godman who blessed his wounded arm and instructed him to serve others as long as he could. Though the arm was lost, Murad Ali soon felt better, and in 1905, he began making his trademark galawat ke kabab in one corner of Chowk, at that time Lucknow's most popular bazaar. The kababs gained popularity not just for their taste and flavour but also for how Murad Ali ran his operations, quite literally, single-handedly. With time, he moved from the shack on the street to a tiny shop, but continued to make the kababs himself. A few tables were later added, but the place remained accessible to even the poorest, while simultaneously being recognized for its nuanced flavour and texture by aficionados of fine food.

After Haji Murad Ali's passing, his nephew, Haji Rais Ahmad, took over the business since the former did not have a son. Ahmad not only ensured that the quality of the kababs remained the same, he did not let prices increase despite rising costs. Himself a great kababchi, Rais Ahmad is said to have expanded the business with skill, honesty, and goodwill. It was also during his time that the establishment started making their immensely popular parathas. Commonly known as Mughlai paratha, this ulte tawe ka paratha is made over an inverted karahi with refined wheat flour, fat, sugar, salt and, some insiders say, even a pinch of custard powder that makes it softer and sweeter. The paratha and kabab with their wholesome flavours and textures form a complete meal that the common man can afford at the end of a hard day. Connoisseurs would travel all the way to Chowk for them.

In an interview a few years ago, the late Nawab Jafar Mir Abdullah, the last of the nawabs, also known as the face of Lucknow's cultural heritage, revealed that he and his friends would visit Tunday Kababi every evening after playing cricket. He mentions how they loved eating the piping hot, tender kababs before heading home. I know of locals, many septuagenarians, who would make regular trips to Tunday.

But since the kabab was made from buffalo meat, it kept away a large section of people who were either uncomfortable or were ritually forbidden from eating buffalo meat kababs. This changed when Mohammad Usman, Haji Rais Ahmad's son, set up his shop in Aminabad in 1995. For the first time, he started making the galawat ke kabab with mutton. This decision opened the restaurant up to more people.

While the original connoisseurs of Tunday ke kabab still frequented Chowk, Usman, today in his late fifties, slowly built an empire of his own. His restaurant at Aminabad, where he only served kabab and paratha, expanded its menu to include qormas, curries, and biryanis. From buffalo meat being the mainstay, mutton became the dominant meat, and popular dishes like tandoori chicken, though not typically Awadhi, were added, to offer more variety. Over the years, even some vegetarian fare like paneer and dals were included. Although not exceptionally good, the vegetarian menu met the needs of the odd vegetarian that landed at Tunday Kababi and demonstrated Usman's inclusivity and alignment with changing times. Today, he runs two other branches in the city, both of which offer the same menu and quality of food.

The outlet at Chowk meanwhile continued to be looked after by Rais Ahmad until he passed away in 2022. Today, it is managed by Mohammad Rizwan, Rais's younger son and Usman's younger brother. Additional offerings did find their way to the menu, but it primarily remains a place where locals stop by for kabab-paratha and not complete meals.

'Despite having just one functional hand, my grandfather worked hard to establish the goodwill that you see today. My father built on this legacy with honesty and hard work. I only try to keep their vision alive,' Mohammad Usman, the grandson of Tunday mian and the current owner of the brand, tells me when I meet him at the Aminabad outlet. I have known Usman Bhai for years now, as a regular consumer, a great fan of their food, and as a journalist, who has closely observed their business model and growing popularity.

I have always noticed his humility above everything else. Despite the patronage of celebrities, politicians, and film stars, and his popularity among the public, there is not a trace of complacency in Usman Bhai. He still comes to the restaurant every day and supervises operations. 'Till he was alive, my father would remind us every day that we should never compromise on our quality even if it affected profits, and we keep true to this commitment even today,' he answers when I ask him about his discipline and dedication.

For someone whose restaurant is rated among the top in the country and the world, Usman is a humble man and attributes his success to the blessings of Allah and the love of the people. He maintains that it is honesty towards their work that has led to the success of Tunday Kababi and believes that the family has been blessed with the responsibility of feeding those in need—taste and popularity are secondary. Perhaps that is why every morning before the place opens to the public, free lunch is distributed among the poor, and every night after shutting, the practice is repeated, ensuring those in need get a meal.

'There is an honesty in his work, and it speaks for itself. The entire family, including the young sons of Usman mian, follow the ethos of their forefathers which was to serve the public and be true to their work,' Professor Pant tells me.

Much of Tunday Kababi's early popularity can be attributed to one man: Jiggs Kalra. A noted journalist, restaurateur, and food researcher, Kalra had discovered the flavours of Tunday's kababs back when few people outside of Lucknow knew of it.

'Jiggs was a great friend and mentor to me. We first met at Chowk when I was a young man, and we instantly became friends,' recalls Usman. He took me with him to the biggest hotels across the world and gave our food a platform we could never imagine.' It was Jiggs who introduced Usman to many film stars. 'Once the late Dilip Kumar tasted our kababs, he became our biggest fan and would invite us over for every party at his place.' If popularity among Bollywood stars is any measure, Tunday Kababi might as well be the most popular place in all of North India, not just Lucknow—from Anil Kapoor to Salman Khan, Dilip Kumar to Dharmendra, Shah Rukh Khan to Aamir Khan, all the big stars have been regular visitors and huge fans.

Despite their popularity across the world neither Usman nor Rizwan have a footprint outside of Lucknow. 'We gave out some franchises a few years ago but realized that they were more interested in making money than maintaining quality and standards, so we withdrew from all of them,' says Usman. Even the name Tunday Kababi comes with its share of claimants. It has often been used by extended family members, even outsiders, trying to cash in on the fame of the establishment while replicating some of their menu within and outside of Lucknow. One such incident in 2014 led to Mohammad Usman filing a lawsuit against Mohammad Muslim, a man who claimed to be Haji Murad Ali's maternal grandson and was therefore entitled to use the name. He had given the franchisee rights to someone in Delhi for a restaurant under the name of 'Lucknow Wale Tunday Kababi'.

In January 2018, following the lawsuit, the Delhi High Court ruled that the name Tunday Kababi legally belongs exclusively to Mohammad Usman, the grandson of Haji Murad Ali. 'My brother Mohammed Rizwan does use the name at the original Chowk outlet, but we are not associated in any way,' says Usman. Ask him why he lets the name be used and Usman only smiles.

An Undisputed Culinary Reputation

One can attribute the popularity and success of Tunday Kababi to many things, but it is the food that remains the primary draw. Whether it is their velvety kabab, the flaky paratha, the layered sheermal, the fragrant qorma, or the delicious biryani, every dish is a testament to the care taken in preserving age-old cooking methods and using traditional recipes that ensure the food turns out excellent day after day.

The kabab is the star of the show here. Legend has it that the proprietary masala used in the kabab is made of more than 300 spices and herbs, though close associates put this number between 140 to 160. A lot of these spices are, in fact, not even spices but herbs, flowers, or roots of various plants that have traditionally been used in Awadhi cuisine—patthar ke phool (black stone flower), khus ki jad (vetiver roots), kali mirch (black pepper), peeli mirch (yellow chilli), and kababchini (tailed pepper or allspice) are some examples. The proportions used in this spice blend are what make it so special and, as expected, it is a closely guarded family secret.

'Our spice mix was first made by my grandfather in consultation with Hakim Safdar Nawab. The recipe was passed down to the women in the family who continued to make it. Till my mother was alive, she was the custodian of the recipe and responsible for making it; now my wife is,' says Usman. No outsider, however loyal a cook or close a relative, has ever been privy to the recipe, and the spice mix is still added to the food by a family member—either Usman or one of his sons—every day. 'The spices used in our kabab were prescribed by a noted Unani hakim (practitioners of alternate medicine who were popular in earlier times and used herbs and spices). They not only add taste and flavour to the food but also aid digestion, increase vigour, and add vitality to the body. Even if you overeat our food, you'll never complain of indigestion,' he elaborates.

'What makes Awadhi cuisine special is not just the masalas we use, but how we use them. People in Lucknow excel at balancing masalas to achieve the right flavours,' explains Taiyaba Ali, a young chef known for bringing

Awadhi cuisine out of Lucknow homes and into upmarket restaurants and star hotels across India. Taiyaba lists major spices like pepper, mace, nutmeg, black cardamom, and rose petal and scents like meetha ittar and screw pine essence that are used in the kababs. She attributes the changing tastes of every establishment and each family to the balance and proportion of the spice mix they use. 'It is the ratio of the spices that determines the taste of a kabab. It is also why some kababs may appeal to your palate more than others.'

Then there is the form. The kababs at Tunday are made with the finest meat that is mixed with 40 per cent fat and minced three times over. It is the fat, and how well it is blended with the mince, that gives the kabab its velvety texture. This mince is tenderized with raw papaya, ginger, and salt, seasoned with the homemade spice blend, mixed with binding agents like gram flour or all-purpose flour, and smoked with a special ghee dhungar (a piece of coal smoked with spices and ghee). The final mixture is shaped into small round patties and grilled on a flat brass lagan over low flame. The fat in the mince ensures the kabab cooks quickly from the inside, and the ghee on top makes it crisp on the outside. The result is a smooth, smoky, soft kabab that is, to use the clichéd but apt phrase, melt-in-your-mouth. Eat it on its own, and it is a filling, flavourful snack; pair it with a paratha, and it becomes a hearty meal. Whether they use buffalo meat or mutton, the recipe for the kababs is the same, Usman explains, but due to the properties of the meat, the buffalo meat kabab, called bade ke kabab, is always softer and more flavourful.

The kabab is the undisputed star at Tunday Kababi, but their biryani and qorma are immensely popular too. The qorma with its earthy, hearty, and layered flavours features the softest pieces of mutton in a smooth, creamy curry made with a generous amount of fried onions and thick creamy yoghurt. Meanwhile, the biryani with its pearly white, spring yellow, and bright orange grains of long basmati rice glistens with fat. The pieces of mutton (or chicken) are so soft that they fall off the bone. Awadhi biryani uses very little, if any, masala and is made primarily with aromatics which make it light and delicate. Here too, the biryani is mild and fragrant. I believe Tunday's biryani is the finest in Lucknow—and the world.

And it's not just me. Tunday Kababi draws people from all over the globe. Whatever else people may know of Lucknow, they all are aware of the restaurant and its legacy.

'I had always heard of Tunday Kababi and its food from my father who would visit Lucknow regularly for work. Growing up, friends too told me how good the food there was, so I came to Lucknow with a lot of hope,' says Aseem Hattangadi a tourism industry professional from Mumbai. 'Popular places often don't live up to the hype but I was blown away by the food at Tunday Kababi. The kabab was so soft that I couldn't hold it without breaking it; the korma was flavourful yet so light on the palate and stomach that I didn't feel stuffed even after eating a lot of it; and the sheermal was sweet, soft, and comforting. The way it soaked all that curry up.... I am salivating just thinking of it,' he adds. Most others who visit the restaurant have the same reaction. 'I now know that versions of Awadhi biryani I have so far been eating were not authentic. The Tunday biryani trumps all,' Aseem says emphatically.

A large part of the crowd in the Aminabad outlet consists of travellers like Aseem. It is no wonder then that just that one outlet sells over 100 kilograms of biryani every day and over 100 kilograms of buffalo meat kababs. The orders for mutton kababs are comparatively fewer and come in at number three along with the mutton qorma.

Keeping Up with the Times

While its lifetime has been long, it is in the past two decades that Tunday Kababi has seen the most rapid growth. This is in terms of footfall, restaurant expansion, and the opening of newer branches. It is also in the awards they have won, a recognition of their legacy worldwide, and the clientele they are reaching today.

'My grandmother used to tell me how the original Tunday Kababi had started with just a small angeethi and a tasla (shallow frying vessel) at the Akbari Gate in Chowk. In a few years, as Tunday mian gained popularity, he moved into a small shop with a few tables but the place was frequented by men—youngsters out for an evening stroll or older men on their way home, stopping for kababs. It was a place where only the common man would eat,' Taiyaba shares.

This started to change in the late 1990s after Usman opened the Aminabad restaurant. However, even until the early 2000s not too many women and families visited. In fact, Taiyaba was not allowed to eat at Tunday Kababi even as recently as 2008 when her father would pack the kababs if the children wanted them.

Even when I started visiting the place in the early 2000s with my husband (before which I too had never ventured to Tunday Kababi despite being a local), I was among the very few women in the restaurant, all of whom, including me, were with their families. Over the past two decades, I have seen this trend change. Not only are there more families—and people from all backgrounds—but many women-only groups are also common.

Debashish believes that there are several factors that could have caused this change. 'One, there is now a dedicated space for families and women, and they are always given seating preference. Secondly, the place is cleaner and air-conditioned. And finally, because eating out has changed drastically in the past few years—one no longer waits for a special occasion. Driven by media and social media, everyone is open to experimenting irrespective of their social or financial background.'

This is certainly the case. Tunday Kababi has evolved to accommodate the changing needs of its customers. Creating more restaurants in different parts of the city, offering home delivery through local partners, taking their food to Lulu Mall, the largest mall in Lucknow, and providing spaces for celebrations, gatherings, and social events for their patrons are some of the ways in which the brand has achieved this feat.

'Our Kapurthala branch is a three-storey building, and each floor has different styles of restaurants. We have a casual cafe, a fine dining space, and a large hall where we can host up to 500 people at a time,' Mohammad Faizan, Usman's son tells me when we speak on the phone. 'We wanted to offer a smart new space to our patrons where they could get the same old flavours but in a stylish ambience. We also wanted to offer an exclusive space for events where we could cater to large gatherings.'

Faizan, along with his brothers Salman, Imran, and Rehan, is responsible for the execution of the expansion and managing the daily workings of all the restaurants. This is also why the company is now investing time and energy in training its existing employees, cooks, and chefs to take charge at other locations. As the chain grows bigger, advancements are being made in technology, systems, and processes to ensure the streamlining of operations and their seamless functioning.

While they are responsible for bringing in new ideas and executing modern business models, the young men haven't lost touch with their roots and strive to keep the ethos of the brand intact. There is a great regard for the past and immense respect for the employees, customers, and partners who, according to Faizan, make them who they are. He tells me, 'I have seen my father work hard every single day of my life, and I want to ensure we can take that legacy forward. But, most of all, we want to make sure we do it the right way without compromising on the values and ethics that make us who we are.'

With so much recognition, many awards, and a clientele that continues to grow, I ask Faizan if they plan to set up outside Lucknow. 'Since the franchisee model has not worked for us, we are now working on a format of company-owned and company-operated restaurants,' he tells me. 'The first one in this series is coming up in Old Delhi, and Inshallah, we will have a few more in other parts of the world also.' The model, he adds, will ensure that the brand is not diluted and the family can keep a close eye on the quality. 'We want to ensure that the taste and experience our customers get across the world remains the same.'

As a patron of Tunday Kababi, an advocate of their food, and an industry insider, I agree with Faizan's point of view and the establishment's approach to the expansion of business. To me—like thousands of locals—it is the repeatability and reproducibility of Tunday Kababi's flavours and textures that set it apart from the other kabab shops in Lucknow where recipes are often compromised and flavours have diluted over time. Even two and a half decades later, every time I return to Tunday Kababi I am assured of the same taste regardless of the time of the day, size of the crowd, or the status of the guest. This, I believe, is their biggest strength—apart from the kabab, of course, the subtle flavour of which lingers on my palate long after I leave the restaurant and beckons me to come back again and again.

Must-have Dishes at Tunday Kababi

Galawat ke kabab

The undisputed star at Tunday Kababi, responsible for the brand's fame and popularity, is the velvety soft galawat ke kabab. The original galawat ke kababs were made with buffalo meat, but now they are also made with mutton. Made with galawat or the tenderizer of raw papaya, these kababs are unique to Lucknow—and especially Tunday. These small, fragrant, and succulent kababs are best eaten on their own, but many locals also prefer having them with the saffron-laced sheermal bread or the ulte tawe ka paratha.

Mutton qorma

The mutton qorma is a quintessential Awadhi dish that is made with a large proportion of yoghurt and the choicest of spices that lend it its mild, layered taste and flavour. While everyone has their own version, the qorma at Tunday Kababi stands out for the smooth gravy and perfectly cooked mutton which almost falls off the bone. The popular way is to eat it with paratha, but you can also mix it with the biryani to experience a completely new flavour. Use a sheermal to soak up the thin curry at the end.

Chicken masala

Tunday was never known for its chicken dishes, but the spicy chicken masala changed that for them. A popular wedding dish, chicken masala may look spicy to the eye, but it is a perfectly balanced dish. The grainy texture that comes from the use of peanuts, khoya (mawa), and gram flour, and the flavour that is enhanced by spices like black pepper and lazzat-e-taam (whole spices like coriander, cumin, clove, pepper, mace, nutmeg, dried rose petals, sandalwood powder, and fennel tied in a small piece of muslin and cooked with the dish), taste best with the ulte tawe ka paratha.

Sheermal

The most indulgent bread in Lucknow, the sheermal at Tunday Kababi looks and tastes absolutely different from the ones you'd find in Delhi or other cities. Made with equal parts milk and flour and a generous amount of ghee, saffron, and ittar, the sheermal can be eaten on its own or with the kabab and qormas. Many regulars make rolls with the sheermal and galawat ke kabab and many use it to mop up the spicy qorma. You can do all three to ensure you make the most of this flaky, soft bread.

Kheer

The only dessert you get at Tunday Kababi is kheer. This North Indian dessert is made from fragrant basmati rice, fresh milk, and sugar, and then scented with screw pine essence, which is widely used in Awadhi cuisine. The mildly sweet and grainy kheer is set in small earthen pots called sakora that lend their earthy flavours to the dessert. Served cold and in small portions, this is a beautiful way to conclude your meal at the restaurant.

NOSTALGIA AND THE MAKING OF A LEGEND

Peter Cat, Kolkata (10)

Priyadarshini Chatterjee

A small map in a rosewood frame sits on my bedside table. The map is of one part of Kolkata's famous thoroughfare—Park Street. A tiny red heart marks a spot on a crisscross of lanes on this map. That red heart is one of Kolkata's most iconic restaurants—Peter Cat.

Peter Cat is where my husband and I met for our first date while we were in college. We sat at a table for two by the wall, to our left, near the foot of the stately staircase that leads to the restaurant's mezzanine floor. We shared a plate of shikar kabab—smoky, spicy chunks of tender goat meat—and goblets of prawn cocktail—succulent prawns in a chilled sweet and sour cocktail sauce of mayonnaise and ketchup that got its zing from lashings of Tabasco, horseradish, and Worcestershire sauce. It's been sixteen years since that July afternoon, and life has changed constantly since. The city has metamorphosed too—physically, culturally, economically, and politically. But inside the walls of Peter Cat, time seems to have frozen.

Peter Cat takes no reservations, and there is almost always a queue outside. On being ushered in, you feel a sense of relief from the harsh Kolkata sun and jubilation at being in this 195-seater restaurant that catapults you back in time.

The interiors are a quirky jumble of Europeanisms and Orientalisms: navy blue carpets rich with damask patterns, textured cream-coloured walls, biophilic accents like leafy plants, red silk pendant lamps that resemble upturned tulips, vinyl seats, and upholstered banquettes. Peter Cat's retro decor has stayed more or less unchanged since its inception.

The same goes for the waiters. Their white pathanis paired with maroon velvet waistcoats accented by golden threads and emerald green, along with long-tailed cream and red turbans seem to hark back to an era gone by.

Inside, the dimly lit interior is suffused by an orange glow. The restaurant is alive with a cadenced murmur. You hear the urgent hissing of sizzlers as liveried waiters carry them ceremoniously to the tables. There is the clink of forks and spoons and the smell of smoke and spices—the restaurant seems to be congealed in time, but that's part of its charm.

A Street Full of History

Park Street has transformed beyond recognition over the past decade. New restaurants and national and international F&B chains have claimed prime spots on the stretch, drastically changing its food tapestry. But Peter Cat remains unchanged. It is a solid tether in the face of life's vicissitudes, a living bridge that connects to a past.

Peter Cat's 18A Park Street address is an iconic one. Stephen Court, the building that houses Peter Cat stands on a corner plot at the intersection of Park Street and

Middleton Row (today known as Sir William Jones Sarani). It is a heritage property intrinsically tied to the city's cosmopolitan history. In the second half of the nineteenth century, Calcutta's Armenian community turned their attention to real estate and played a massive role in shaping the city's skyline. For instance, the Armenian real estate baron, Johannes Carapiet Galstaun, built over 300 structures around the city including Park Street's historic Queens Mansion. Stephen Court was built by Armenian jeweller-turned-real-estate-mogul Arathoon Stephen, who owned other Calcutta landmarks like the Grand Hotel (today The Oberoi Grand), Empire Theatre (it no longer exists), and the majestic Mount Everest Hotel in Darjeeling (which has since been demolished).

Stephen Court houses a mix of private apartments and commercial spaces, including a bunch of vintage Park Street eateries like Flurys, Kolkata's famous tearoom started by the Swiss couple Joseph and Freida Flury and their compatriot Quinto Cinzio Trinca in 1927. It is also home to One Step Up, which specializes in Kolkata's trademark continental food. 'The spot that Peter Cat occupies was previously a godown that belonged to the Calcutta Customs where confiscated goods were stored,' says founder and owner Nitin Kothari, a handsome man with a soft, cadenced voice and sharp eyes that sparkle from behind his slim spectacles. Now in his seventies, Kothari is a name to reckon with in the city's restaurant and business circuit. Regulars to Peter Cat know him because he is usually at the restaurant in the evenings.

The entrance to the restaurant is on Middleton Row, a vibrant street, although off the main thoroughfare, rich in history and home to many heritage buildings. At No. 1 Middleton Row, for instance, stands the Gallway House (YWCA hostel and guest house). Its foundation stone was laid in 1925 by the Countess of Lytton. Further down the road is the nineteenth-century St Thomas Roman Catholic Church and Loreto House School and College. This reputed educational institution was started by Irish nuns from Loreto Island in what was once the garden house of Sir Elijah Impey, and before him several other luminaries of Bengal's colonial government. The lane where Peter Cat stands today served as the private carriage drive, a tree-lined avenue stretching from the main road to Sir Elijah's grand mansion. Historian P. Thankappan Nair says Park Street, previously called Burial Ground Road or Badamtallee, gets its name from Sir Elijah's sprawling gardens that were akin to public parks.

Was There a Cat Named Peter?

Peter Cat opened its doors in 1975.

'Initially, I wanted to name the restaurant Omar Khayyam. But then it wasn't catchy enough. So we went with Peter Cat, a name that popped into my mind out of nowhere and stayed,' shares Nitin. It also helped that the name was cuisine agnostic, as Peter Cat would eventually go the multi-cuisine route. Nitin confirms there was no cat named Peter that inspired the name. However, the disposable paper table mats in shades of neon pink, green, and orange feature a grumpy cat, and the menus are in the shape of a cat's face. Yet the name, in a sense, is serendipitous. The land on which Stephen Court was built was originally owned by a Peter Charles Earnest Paul. The name of the restaurant then is an inadvertent hat tip to the first owner of the plot.

'The original idea was to serve up wholesome Mughlai food—the biryani-chaap-roti routine—in a well-appointed and hygienic space, as opposed to the no-frills, often shabby establishments that typically served such food at the time,' Nitin tells me. So, when he opened doors to his restaurant, the highlights of the menu were mutton and chicken chaap and handkerchief-thin roomali rotis to mop up the rich gravies.

Long before kitchen theatres became a buzzword, Nitin had introduced a show kitchen at his restaurant. Behind its glass wall, massive pans of chicken and mutton chaap simmered away invitingly. A touch of theatre was added by the roomali roti experts who entertained diners with their skills of flipping and throwing the rolled out rotis into the air in order to shape it, before slapping it on an upturned kadhai. But as demand increased, space became a constraint, and Nitin had to close it down for a larger kitchen. The upper mezzanine floor laid out with a mix of square and round tables with a revolving centre for condiments was also added. That revolving table centre had me hooked as a child.

The menu also expanded. 'It often happened that of four diners, at least one would want a soup or a roast chicken. I decided to add more options to the menu so no guest was dissatisfied,' says Nitin. Rising to the wants of their diners is a recurrent theme in the success story of Peter Cat.

The Beginnings

The story of Peter Cat began long before Nitin Kothari established the restaurant in Calcutta. It began with his father, Shivji V. Kothari.

The Kotharis are originally from Kutch in Gujarat. But for generations, the family lived in Karachi in present-day Pakistan and a part of the Bombay Presidency during the Raj. This was until the Partition forced them to leave their homes behind. Nitin was, in fact, born in Karachi. 'We first moved to Bombay (now Mumbai) in 1947, where my father secured a catering contract for the Santacruz Airport restaurant that served both crew and passengers. He also set up the first flight kitchen of independent India that catered onboard meals to all airlines flying out from Bombay.' However, Calcutta was a bustling metropolis—the place to be at that time. The airport in Calcutta saw more traffic, and the city served as a stopover on the London–Tokyo sector. Shivji decided to move to Calcutta in 1949. Seven years later, in the summer of 1956, he opened the doors to what would become one of Park Street's most legendary culinary addresses, Mocambo, a few hundred meters away from where Peter Cat would come up later.

'Park Street was the Champs-Élysées of the East,' remembers Nitin, describing the halcyon days of the thoroughfare once well known as the city's cabaret row. A visit to Park Street to wine and dine at one of its numerous restaurants and nightclubs was never a casual affair. 'Men would be dressed in dinner jackets or linen suits, and women in stunning gowns. You couldn't be seen dead on Park Street in the wrong clothes.' And above all was Park Street's legendary live music scene that some claim was the best in Asia at the time. Park Street's restaurants and bars were an oasis for bands, musicians, and cabaret acts. Jazz and alcohol flowed freely, and everyone was happy.

Of course, there were a few unsavoury spots scattered in the lanes and bylanes around its edges. Mocambo's location was previously a seedy sailor's bar named Kohinoor. There were others on the street like Isaiah. 'In the 1950s, Calcutta was still a thriving port where numerous ships docked, and there were several such watering holes that hosted sailors who came ashore. But my father wanted to build a place that was a sophisticated, posh nightclub. He stripped the place down to its bones and built it from scratch with the help of a German architect,' Nitin explains. Today people flock to Mocambo for their creamy devilled crab, chicken à la kiev gravy with molten butter, and fish à la Diana, an extravagant dish of Bengal bhekti (Asian seabass) stuffed with prawns and simmered in a cream-laden sauce. But back then revellers trickled in for Mocambo's famed cabaret acts and the intoxicating voice of Pam Crain who performed with Anton Menezes's six-piece band. 'My father called Mocambo the first nightclub in India. He even had a glass dance floor designed with coloured psychedelic lights fitted underneath.'

Nitin recalls how 'at the time Italians were considered the best in the restaurant and food business'. Historian Antonella Viola confirms this in her essay 'Italian Traders in Bengal, 1850–1950': 'Perhaps the most well-known Italians in Bengal and all over India were those who worked in the hospitality industry; Italian confectioners and caterers who had opened up restaurants and hotels were particularly appreciated in colonial India.' So Shivji employed an Italian manager who drew up Mocambo's original menu, much of which remains unchanged.

It was here at Mocambo that Nitin would be initiated

into the food business. He went to boarding school in the hills of Darjeeling at the renowned St. Paul's School. 'We had three long months of winter break,' he recollects. But vacations were not all fun and games. 'My father was a hard taskmaster and he insisted that my vacations be spent learning the ropes of the culinary business. Much of my vacation was spent toiling in the kitchen at Mocambo.'

Nitin's restaurant arrived on the scene during a period of transition for the city. In the late 60s, while the rest of Bengal and Calcutta reeled (and bled) under Naxalite violence, Park Street remained immune for the most part, wrapped in a cocoon of gaiety. As Sumanta Banerjee writes in his book *In the Wake of Naxalbari* (1980), 'In the posh areas of Park Street and Chowringhee gathered all the gaiety and frivolity of the city. Swanky business executives and thriving journalists, film stars and art critics, smugglers and touts, chic society dames and jet-set teenagers thronged the bars and discotheques. All mention of the rural uprising in these crowds was considered distinctly in bad taste, although the term Naxalite had assumed an aura of the exotic and was being used to dramatize all sorts of sensationalism in these circles—ranging from good-natured Bohemianism to hippy-style pot sessions.'

By the time Peter Cat came on the scene, the Park Street of 'good times' was rapidly morphing into a shadow of its past. Two years after Peter Cat opened its doors, the CPI (M)-led Left Front government came to power in Bengal. One of its early casualties was Park Street's unparalleled live music scene, terminated by the government's prohibitive tax on live entertainment, a bourgeoisie indulgence the communist government staunchly disapproved of. 'By the 70s, most of the live music acts had wound down, and the focus was solely on food. And Peter Cat delivered,' tells Kolkata-based culinary enthusiast and writer Rukshana Kapadia.

'And yet Peter Cat for me is deeply entwined with Park Street, the OG high street of India that I grew up on. A restaurant that focuses solely on its food and retained its menu without changes for decades is a shining example of a legacy among the multi-cuisine restaurants of Kolkata. I think Peter Cat made North Indian kababs and curries chic for an entire generation in the 70s,' says Rukshana, adding that their tandoor dishes were also a rage.

Peter Cat's Chelo Kabab

The dish that Peter Cat is known for is of Iranian descent—the chelo kabab.

In 1965, Nitin went to study hotel management in Salzburg, Austria. After he graduated, he moved to Frankfurt, Germany, to work in the kitchens of the

German airlines Lufthansa as a chef and to train in the intricacies of running a kitchen that could cater to in-flight dining at scale. After a three-year stint, Nitin returned to Calcutta via Iran. It was in Tehran, a pit stop to meet friends, that he chanced upon what would be the recipe for his future success. 'My friends in Tehran took me out for a meal of what they called chelo. What arrived was a massive sharing platter of piping hot rice and smoking hot beef kababs. Our host took a mound of butter and added it to the rice. Next, he cracked a few raw eggs into the rice and mixed it all up with his bare hands,' explains Nitin.

Najmieh Batmanglij, in the book *Food of Life: A Book of Ancient Persian and Modern Iranian Cooking and Ceremonies*, writes, 'Chelo kabab is Iran's national dish, the equivalent of meat and potatoes in America. It's eaten in every household, regardless of social class; it can be found everywhere, from palaces to stalls in the bazaar. But the best chelo kababs are probably those sold in the bazaars'. Originally, the chelo kabab comprised fragrant rice moistened with butter and kabab-e-koobideh, flattened batons of gently seasoned minced meat cooked on skewers. Knobs of butter and chargrilled tomatoes are often served alongside, and a generous sprinkling of sumac elevates the dish. Raw eggs are added sometimes.

'The dish fascinated me and I tucked it in the recesses of my mind. Later, when I opened my restaurant, I put it on the menu, albeit tweaked to local tastes and preferences,' Nitin adds.

Peter Cat's version of the chelo kabab, listed under the 'Aphrodisiacs from the Harem' (although no one has confirmed its aphrodisiacal virtues) section of the menu and described as 'the protected regional product of West Bengal', is a plated meal comprising rice and two kinds of kababs—slender cylinders of minced meat seekh kababs freckled with spices and herbs like mint and coriander, and smoky brochettes of mutton or chicken chunks laced with a nut-enriched marinade. This is interspersed with onions, tomatoes, and capsicums. Grilled tomatoes and sliced cucumbers are served alongside. A few small cubes of cold butter sit on top of a bed of fluffy, pristine white rice. The blobs are supposed to melt into the rice but usually need a little nudge. There is also a soft fried egg with an oozy centre that streams out in golden rivulets.

Exotic yet underpinned by a comforting familiarity, this culinary amalgamation quite easily appealed to Kolkata's Bengali gentry that comprised the major chunk of Peter Cat's customer base. 'The Bengali love for buttered rice could easily rival, in fact, surpass the Japanese love for it,' says blogger and writer Poorna Banerjee. 'They also love the combination of rice and meat (or other protein),' she adds.

In the Bong (an ethnic slur turned badge of pride for the modern urban middle-class Bengali) imagination, chelo kabab is as much a part of their own culinary repertoire as the bhetki paturi (thick slices of Asian seabass sheathed in a pungent mustard-rich marinade, wrapped in banana leaves, and then steamed or fried). Chelo kabab's exclusivity was its chief draw. For decades the dish remained within the confines of the restaurant. In fact, in Calcutta, it is synonymous with the place.

'A gentleman who had been dining at Peter Cat for years travelled to Tehran where his Iranian associates took him out for chelo kabab. The man not only dissed the Iranian original, but when the associates came to Calcutta, he brought them to Peter Cat to give them a taste of what he called the "real" chelo kabab,' Nitin shares. 'I was at the restaurant then, squirming in my seat. I didn't try to find out his guests' reaction to the dish,' he laughs. These days restaurants across the city have started putting the dish on the menu, but many diners consider them imitations of the Peter Cat original. It is safe to say the dish has morphed into a cultural hallmark.

But why should meat-loving Bengalis have all the fun? 'Vegetarian guests at the restaurant who had heard about the chelo kabab wanted a vegetarian version. So, we put it on the menu,' says Nitin. The vegetarian chelo comes with spiced and grilled squares of soft paneer, seekh kabab made with minced veggies and lentils, and a massive potato sheathed in a bright orange marinade, stuffed with spices, and then roasted in a tandoor. Some would say that the vegetarian chelo is sacrilege. One X (formerly Twitter) user even tweeted that his cousin broke up with a boy for suggesting she eat a vegetarian chelo at Peter Cat. But to be fair, it's a decent dish.

The second most ordered dish at Peter Cat is perhaps a sizzler. There's hardly anyone who hasn't scalded their tongue at Peter Cat as they dived impatiently into their sizzler. There are several options on the menu. The chicken steak sizzler has plump, batter-coated minced chicken patties and thick-cut potato fries luxuriating in a glossy brown sauce and served with a fried egg and fat batons of blanched carrots and green beans on a partially singed bed of cabbage leaves. There is the tandoori mixed grill sizzler that has a motley crew of spiced and chargrilled proteins—prawns, chicken, and mutton—doused in a decidedly North Indian gravy that comes to the table brown and seething.

More Than Its Chelo Kabab and Sizzlers

The more discerning patrons of Peter Cat will tell you that chelo kabab, although the most popular dish here, is an uninspired choice. Some would even call the dish vastly overrated. Those in the know will tell you that Peter Cat's menu is studded with a few other gems that far outshine the chelo or the sizzlers that most people order.

One such dish is the dum ki raan. For this dish, the whole leg of a young goat is covered in a yoghurt-based marinade rich with fragrant spices and alliums for over twenty-four hours. The marinated leg is then stuck into a tandoor and slow-cooked until the meat is succulent and tender, but still retains its shape and meaty texture. The leftover marinade is cooked down to an indulgent gravy until it is deliciously caramelized. The meat is pulled off the bone in juicy shreds, and they are tossed in the gravy and served with panache on a salver. Earlier, the dish was presented with a long bone shank tucked in. This added a hint of theatrics and indicated that you were being served an entire leg. 'But we don't serve the bone any more because it made some diners queasy,' says Nitin. The menu also offers a sizzling version of the dish.

Rukshana, who went to college at Loreto nearby reminisces, 'During our college days we dropped in at Peter Cat for lunch at least three to four times a week. My college lunch break was between noon and one, and Peter Cat only opened at 12.30. But they let us in early so we could finish lunch and rush back to college. We even had a fixed table on the upper floor on the left corner and a fixed order of chicken bharta, chicken reshmi butter masala, and some naan to mop up the gravies with,' she says.

Poorna, on the other hand, says, 'When I accompanied my father to Peter Cat as a child, we hardly ever ordered the chelo kabab. Instead, we went for their Indian dishes. They make some of the best fish kababs.' The fish makhmali kabab—chunks of spice-laced fish grilled in the tandoor that is, true to its name, buttery soft and flaky—is easily one of their best dishes.

'It's one of my favourites,' says restaurateur Azmeen Tangri, whose family owns another Park Street institution, Olypub (previously The Olympian Bar), a coming-of-age site for many generations of Calcuttans. Azmeen has grown up closely observing the machinations of Kolkata's original food street. 'Growing up, Peter Cat was our regular haunt. Recently, when a friend who had relocated to Canada long ago returned to the city and we planned to catch up, we simply knew it could be nowhere but at Peter Cat. We landed up there without even spelling it out,' she says.

I too have spent numerous afternoons in line on the pavement outside Peter Cat.

A friend (that I have now lost touch with) and I ordered our first alcoholic drink at Peter Cat, and once in a while lit up a cigarette (it was allowed in the 2000s) just for style, all the while terrified of being caught by someone who knew our families. I had a fixed order too, and it wasn't chelo kabab. Instead, I went for their cold chicken and salad. The dish comprises a hillock of assorted vegetable macédoine laced with a creamy mayo-based dressing and topped with thin escalopes of cold roasted chicken. The dish comes crowned with slender curls of carrots and cucumber. I typically paired it with soft, warm dinner rolls.

Ayan Ghosh, a cigar-smoking globetrotter well known in Kolkata's epicurean circles for his love for porcine treats and his crisp baritone, shares my love for Peter Cat's salads. Ayan remembers visiting Peter Cat as a child with his parents in the late 70s and early 80s: 'My most vivid memory is olfactory. A distinct smell of tobacco smoke, alcohol, and expensive perfume. There was something glamorous about it. Walking up the broad staircase, as your feet sank into the thick carpet, infused in you a sense of regality. The mezzanine floor was the family section then.'

'I have a special penchant for their tutti frutti ice cream,' says Ayan. The tutti frutti sundae is a Park Street staple and perhaps the bestselling dessert at most of Park Street's vintage restaurants. But according to Ayan, Peter Cat's version is a textural treat like few others.

For Kolkata-based marketing professional Shikhar Kapoor, even their chanachur, a snack mix made with deep-fried peanuts, gram, and strands of chickpea batter served with drinks, is special. 'Growing up, I often dined at Peter Cat with my family. I always hoped my father and uncle would order drinks so I could polish off the bowl of chanachur that came with them,' he laughs. 'Our chanachur is customized for us according to our specifications. We tell our vendors the exact proportion of each ingredient in the mixture,' says Nitin.

'I tend to introduce things I like personally. And I have a weakness for sausages. So, for many years, we served a complimentary plate of cocktail pork sausages to our guests with their drinks. Years down the line, we discontinued this because a part of our clientele had reservations,' he adds. Though the sausage platter is gone, the menu features a few scrumptious bites to go with a tipple. A hot pick is the chicken liver masala, chunks of perfectly cooked liver sheathed in a feisty masala.

Looking Forward Always

Some of Park Street's most popular addresses are owned by the Kotharis. While Nitin runs Mocambo and Peter Cat, his elder brother, the late Shailendra Shivji Kothari, fondly called Baba Kothari, and now his sons, own another Park Street hotspot, BarBQ, its adjoining Chinese specialty restaurant, Flavours of China, and the quaint One Step Up across the street.

A tragic fire in 2007 damaged Flavours of China. Three years later, in 2010, another terrible fire broke out in Stephen Court that resulted in several tragic deaths and brought the entire city to a halt.

'We were running a full house when news of the fire raging through the upper floors of the building reached us. It's an old building and such incidents have occurred in the past. So, at first, we were unperturbed.

But soon we realized that the intensity of the fire was unprecedented,' Nitin recalls. 'We had to rush people out of the restaurant in the middle of their meal. Even then, some people insisted on finishing their food and others on paying even as we announced that we were waiving the bills,' he adds.

The building, ravaged by the fire, its soot-stained walls and broken pillars a haunting reminder of the tragedy, was sealed off for weeks. During this time the restaurant was off-limits to the Kotharis. 'When we were finally allowed to enter weeks later, the whole place was in a shambles—damaged by water and foam, used perhaps as a precautionary measure as the fire hadn't reached the lower levels. It was a harrowing time, but we worked together to put things back in place. The day we opened the doors to our restaurant again, we were pleasantly surprised to see customers streaming in as if nothing had happened,' says Nitin.

But the deadly fire was only one of the many challenges that Kothari faced over the decades. The initial years, for instance, were rather trying, particularly due to the mounting labour problems resulting from continuous strife with labour unions. The newly elected Left Front regime presided over an abysmal crisis in industrial relations and an unchallenged rise in militant trade unionism resulting in an exodus of capital from the state.

'Until the 1960s West Bengal was the most

industrialized state in the country, but one by one all our major industries moved out. In Kolkata, numerous restaurants fell prey to this militant unionism,' says Nitin. The older generations in Kolkata still mourn the fall of Park Street giants like Sky Room and Blue Fox to the labour crisis. 'The biggest problem was that of discipline—the backbone of the restaurant business. Union leaders goaded workers to completely eschew workplace discipline and ethics. But we stuck it out and managed to sail through, albeit with much difficulty.'

Nitin takes pride in his relationship with his staff, many of whom have worked with him for decades. His first chief cook, who led the kitchen at Peter Cat since its inception, remained in his employment for years past his retirement age. 'I insisted he stay with us, even when he was no longer able to work around the kitchen. Instead, we placed a chair for him in the kitchen and requested him to simply be there. To me, his presence was crucial. It's only a couple of years ago when his health started failing that we let him go. But we keep in touch.'

During the pandemic when many restaurants were forced to lay off their staff, the Kotharis decided to retain their entire staff on almost full salary. In retrospect, Kothari believes it was the best decision. 'When the pandemic was finally over, many restaurants struggled through the ordeal of recruiting fresh staff and training them. We had an advantage as we had our entire staff on hand, ready to get things going at once.' Kothari's commitment to his staff is only perhaps surpassed by his commitment to his guests.

Peter Cat's greatness doesn't depend on name-brand chefs or flashy food trends or show-stopping innovation. It rides on the strength of a winning combination of inexpensive alcohol and dependable, affordable, and comforting food cocooned in nostalgia. But what makes Peter Cat truly special is that it is a palimpsest of memories. Through its resilience, it offers a sense of solidity against the continuous slippage of time and preserves special memories that could otherwise blur. It is in a sense a homecoming at a time when the idea of home is fluid and fragile.

Must-have Dishes at Peter Cat

Chelo kabab

Peter Cat's most famous dish, this is a complete meal by itself. Cubes of soft butter melt into a bed of fragrant rice, flanked by two kinds of smoky, moist kababs: spice-flecked sheesh kababs and brochettes of meat coated in a feisty marinade and chargrilled. To top it off, there's a soft sunny side up.

Fish makhmali kabab

Easily one of the best dishes on the menu, the dish comprises fat chunks of fresh fish laced with a creamy marinade—a blend of yoghurt, spices, and herbs—and grilled to smoky perfection. True to its name the fish is buttery soft and flakes like a dream. Paired with slabs of raw onions and a piquant chutney, it is a plate of soft indulgence.

Prawn cocktail

Succulent shrimps are poached in a flavourful court bouillon and dressed in a silken, spunky sweet, and tart sauce, a pale peach in colour, made with mayonnaise, fresh cream, ketchup, a dash of Worcestershire sauce, and a drizzle of Tabasco pepper sauce and seasoning. It gets its distinct zing from a touch of horseradish sauce.

Beckty meunière

A reminder of the city's colonial past, these are batter coated fillets of beckty, a Bay of Bengal delicacy, smothered with herbed cream sauce. It is served with potatoes tossed in a sticky sauce and blanched vegetables.

Tandoori mixed grill sizzler

Bringing together two of Peter Cat's most signature offerings—tandoori specialities and sizzlers—this dish is a combination of chargrilled proteins coated in a distinctly North Indian sauce and served sizzling and seething on an iron plate.

THE DHABA THAT BIRTHED A TOWN

Amrik Sukhdev Dhaba, Murthal (16)

OM ROUTRAY

It is the first week of October in Delhi as I sit down to write the story of Amrik Sukhdev Dhaba. There is a slight nip in the morning air. The nip that makes a significant proportion of the city's residents crave a piping hot stuffed paratha and a steaming kulhad (earthen cup) of chai. On weekends, they will get into their cars and head towards Murthal, a highway stop 60 kilometres outside Delhi, a stretch dotted with dhabas, long rows of them. Most of them will aim for a table at Amrik Sukhdev Dhaba, one of the oldest and most iconic in the region.

The story of Amrik Sukhdev has never been told. Apart from the name of the founder and year of establishment, there is no other information in the public domain. When I asked around for ways to get in touch with the family, no one knew how. The famous street food bloggers did not know anyone there. The industry association did not have their details. It seemed everyone knew of them, but no one knew them. It looked like they were trying to stay away from the limelight. Or so I thought until I connected with the fourth-generation owner on LinkedIn, not the usual platform to get in touch with a restaurant owner.

Within hours of making contact, I was on the phone with Suraj Singh, grandson of the founder Prakash Singh, and I realized that the secrecy was not wilfully maintained. Suraj told me how most of the food bloggers who covered the establishment never got in touch, and the few who tried were shooed away by the staff. He was on LinkedIn to make it easier for people to reach him.

A few days later, I was sitting in the posh reception of Home In, a hotel owed by the proprietors of Amrik Sukhdev Dhaba. A row of hotel-branded cars was parked outside. The place was new and rather exclusive. I could have been sitting in the lobby of a luxury apartment building in Gurugram.

As you enter Amrik Sukhdev from the highway, you notice the row of iron barricades that separate the property from the service lane. They were put in place during the Covid years and have now become a traffic management feature. You park and walk past the massive building that houses the restaurant to reach Home In, the shiny new hotel at the back. The parking lot is huge and would entice any real estate developer. One could build a gigantic mall in that space. The guards are helpful, and it is easier to find a spot on weekdays. The building itself is imposing and the logo is familiar. But before you reach the entrance, there are enough distractions. On your left is a Turkish ice cream shop. On your right, a row of chaat counters. During hot and humid summer days, massive humidifiers add more moisture to the outdoor seating area.

And then there is Amrik Sukhdev Dhaba, the reason I was there. I enter and see an endless sea of tables, rows and rows of people waiting or eating, and busy servers constantly looking for empty chairs to seat the incoming crowd. Though every cog in the entire establishment is geared towards feeding you and at great speed, people do not come here just to eat. Even on an incredibly hot day, there will be people milling around the entrance, taking selfies, posing for photographs, and generally idling. I spotted a senior couple sitting comfortably in front of the humidifier, with two kulhads of chai and a giant golden retriever asleep at their feet. Here, great hurry meets the great rest.

Back at the reception of Home In, the wait was short. We were ushered into the office where Amrik Singh and his son, Suraj Singh, were waiting for us. Originally planned for two hours, the interview ran for well over four.

The Accidental Legacy

Amrik Singh's uncle, Sardar Lakshman Singh, ran a dhaba in Miller Ganj, near Ludhiana in Punjab, around 260 kilometres from Murthal. It was popular among truck drivers and business was thriving. He did not have a son, but his sisters did. He asked one of his two sisters who had four sons to allow him to adopt one (unofficially; this was common practice in India in those times). This is how Prakash Singh, her youngest son, arrived to help his uncle run the dhaba at Miller Ganj. All was going well. So well that his second sister asked Sardar Lakshman

Singh to take on her son, Lal Singh, too. Prakash Singh and Lal Singh came to run the dhaba together.

But before long, the cousins had a falling out, and Sardar Lakshman Singh had to work out a solution. He decided that Prakash would be given a new dhaba to run at another location, while Lal Singh would continue working alongside Lakshman Singh in Miller Ganj.

The search for a new place began. Truck drivers, loyal customers as they were, came to the rescue. They told the family that there weren't good places on the outskirts of Delhi where they could take a break and get some food and rest. They suggested Murthal as the ideal highway stop. Further consultations were held, and it was decided that Prakash Singh would head to Murthal to set up his own dhaba.

The year was 1956. Haryana had not yet been created. So when Prakash Singh landed at Murthal, he was still in Punjab. There was only a small, nameless dhaba (as was the norm back then, dhabas did not have names) operating somewhere nearby. For those unfamiliar with the locality, it is impossible to imagine what Murthal would have looked like back then. Independent India was not even a decade old. Delhi was still taking shape. The land for Chanakyapuri, the diplomatic enclave, had just been allocated. Greater Kailash did not exist. Setting up an eatery in Murthal would not have seemed as self-evident as it does now.

Murthal falls on the Grand Truck Road (G. T. Road), one of the oldest and longest trade routes in Asia. G. T. Road extended from Chittagong in present-day Bangladesh to Kabul in Afghanistan. Since the third century BCE, the road has been a vital artery for trade and transport. So while Murthal had not so far become a rest stop, it was not impossible to imagine that it might happen.

Now coming back to Prakash Singh, who rented a small place in Murthal Khas for his dhaba. It was 3 or 4 kilometres away from where Amrik Sukhdev stands today. He and his wife began living in a small room upstairs, while the dhaba operated on the ground floor. Thanks to his network of truck drivers, business began picking up. The menu was simple. Rotis, dal, and three kinds of parathas: potato, onion, and a mix of the two. Within weeks, he began to sell out. The good run continued for a few years, till his landlord wanted to raise the rent. Having established his business by now, Prakash Singh decided to move on and find a place of his own.

In the early 1960s, Prakash Singh bought a piece of land a few hundred metres away from the first dhaba. He built his dhaba in the front and his home was located at the back. A door separated the two sections. Truck drivers began to stop for more than just the food. They bathed, slept on the coir beds, relaxed, and enjoyed their teas.

Amrik was born in 1967. Prakash was a happy man. Life and business were running smoothly. This was probably the longest period of calm that the business and family would ever see.

A Move, an Expansion

Let's move forward to 1982. India was hosting the ninth Asian Games. Delhi underwent monumental infrastructure development, with five new stadia (including the swanky Jawaharlal Nehru stadium) being built, twelve existing ones being renovated and expanded, seven flyovers being constructed, and around thirty roads being widened. A total of 3,411 athletes from thirty-three nations had descended on the capital. The games marked the first colour broadcast in India by Doordarshan. The opening ceremony was attended by nearly 75,000 people. It was a glorious year for Delhi and India.

It also impacted Prakash Singh and his dhaba. The two-lane highway that it was on was widened to four lanes. The parking area was handed over to the highway. After almost two decades of smooth sailing, he had to move again. But this would be his last move. There would be other challenges to tackle but having to find a new location would not be one of them.

Prakash Singh rented an old eatery for ₹300 a month and moved his establishment lock, stock, and chulha to this new site. Its existing structure became the drawing room, and the house was extended to accommodate a growing family. Prakash was now ready to grow roots. For the next thirteen years, the dhaba ran without a glitch. This gave Prakash the stability and resources to plan his next steps.

In 1995, he purchased the land and the building he had been renting and began constructing his biggest project yet—a newer and bigger Amrik Sukhdev Dhaba. All through that time, the kitchen never stopped working, and food was served every day. As we will see later, this commitment continues to be the driving force behind the brand. No matter what happened, food was made and people were fed, every single day. It took five years to complete construction and for the restaurant to open its doors.

A New Century, a New Approach

It was the turn of the century, the year 2000. The new dhaba was inaugurated. Truck drivers were still the most loyal customers, and Prakash Singh's business was geared to serve them. Having spent decades catering to and being around truckers, he knew their needs better than anyone else.

Amrik recalls how his father was the first to invest in private and well-maintained bathrooms for the truck drivers. These were fashioned on the typical Punjabi haudi, irrigation channels in farms where people also bathed. Granite chips were used to embellish the channel, and it was the talk of the town back then. This offered a luxury bathing experience for weary truckers. Amrik Sukhdev remained loyal to the truck drivers the way they had remained loyal to the dhaba.

This was a time when truck stops and private car stops were clearly distinguishable from each other. One could still spot masseurs walking around with bottles of oil. They were 'experts' at bringing relief to bodies ravaged by hours and hours of manoeuvring trucks. But if you did not drive trucks, you went to them only at your own risk. I made the mistake once. Their sinewy hands felt as if they were made of steel. The pressure they applied per square centimetre of human flesh could not have been recommended by any doctor. They found muscles to pull and pinch in the oddest places. It felt painful at the time and got only worse over the next three days. How hard a truck driver's life must be that he found relief in this torture!

But times were changing. Nearly a decade after the economic liberalization of 1991, India was booming. Highways were wider and smoother than ever before. There was an increase in private cars on these roads. While Amrik Sukhdev focused on truck drivers, these cars began stopping at other dhabas in the vicinity that were intent on catering exclusively to families and keen on attracting them. Family dhabas were becoming increasingly luxurious, while dhabas for truck drivers remained the ramshackle huts that they always were. A great opportunity was close to being lost.

Once again, it was a truck driver who came forward to help. A regular at the dhaba, one time he came with his wife and children. He saw drivers sprawled about and felt uncomfortable bringing his family here. He walked up to Prakash Singh, complimented him on the great facilities that he had built, and said the place was great for truck drivers 'who did not deserve such a fine place'. The man then went on to suggest that the new building would be perfect for the private cars zipping past and that Prakash should focus on getting them to stop there.

Murthal of the early 2000s was very different from the Murthal that Prakash Singh had arrived at almost half a century earlier. There were many more dhabas and way more traffic. It had grown to become more than just a pitstop. It was becoming a weekend spot for Delhiites who drove out in hordes for parathas and chai. Prakash realized that Amrik Sukhdev was losing out on a huge opportunity.

Prakash got some business cards printed and headed to the international airport in New Delhi (Amritsar in Punjab began international flights only in 2005). A large number of people from the state of Punjab emigrated in search of greener pastures (a 2023 *India Today* news report estimated 4.78 lakh Punjabis between 2016 and 2021). All such expats frequently visit their families back home in Punjab.

While the dhaba was originally set up fifty years ago to cater to transporters of cargo that drove along the route, now the business pivoted to feed those people who travelled via Delhi on their way to Punjab. They were going after the Indians that everyone in the country wanted as their customers—the non-resident Indians (NRIs). Assurances of free food and generous tips to airport cabbies also helped. Many cab drivers who were once truckers also knew the Amrik Sukhdev Dhaba well.

The NRIs landed. They loved the clean and segregated restrooms and spread the word. The promotions and the food clicked. The pivot was successful. The boom that Amrik Sukhdev Dhaba was experiencing was felt by others in Murthal too. The rising tide had lifted all boats. So far, the restaurants had been flying under the radar. But soon they would need to clear compliances and get certifications from the government to continue operating.

A Demolition and a Fire

Shortly, notices started coming in. Almost everyone ignored them and then fought them. But it was not a battle they could have won. Before long, a demolition notice arrived. The dhaba owners went to the Supreme Court and lost. They appealed to the then chief minister, Bhupinder Singh Hooda, but to no avail.

It was the morning of 18 March 2007. Despite the ongoing tussle with the government, it was business as usual at Amrik Sukhdev. Parathas were in the tandoor, masala tea was brewing on the chulha, and customers were enjoying the last days of winter. Seven JCB machines rolled in with a string of government officials. Within hours Amrik Sukhdev was turned to rubble, as were most eateries in the neighbourhood.

The demolitions set the stage for the next phase of growth, this time with the necessary certifications and compliances in place. The giant buildings that stretched for miles on both sides of the highway would have been impossible without the legal tussle, the demolitions, and subsequently, the clear implementation of the law that began in 2007. Once dhabas entered the formal economy, new investments poured in. But the issue of compliance and the threat of demolitions never really left Murthal because of several complex land-related issues. Sonipat Municipal Corporation served demolition notices to fifty-three dhabas in Murthal in 2018. A hundred more were served to others in the district. The bone of contention was the Change of Land Use (CLU) permissions, the same law under which dhabas had been demolished a decade earlier.

Back in 2007, due to a pile of rubble that was in their way, the JCBs that demolished Amrik Sukhdev could not reach the far side of the building where the restrooms were located. While the application for CLU and labour law compliance issues raged on, the immediate concern for Amrik Sukhdev was how they were going to start serving food, and fast. Someone was dispatched to the nearby villages and a tent house brought in. Within three days, bamboo poles were put up and a massive white tent was standing where the rubble was, complete with large fans and lights. And just like that, within seventy-two hours, Amrik Sukhdev Dhaba was up and running again.

Amrik Singh becomes emotional as he recalls that that within thirty minutes of reopening, all the tables were occupied and there was a queue of customers. He tells me how the brothers couldn't control their tears as they attended to waiting customers and served parathas that day.

Once the permission from CLU was received, the construction of a new building began. This is the structure that we see today. Such was its magnitude that it took seven years, from 2007 to 2014, to complete. All this time, the dhaba operated from a tent.

Rains were a problem, and one time the tent was blown away in a storm. It was then replaced with a waterproof one. Things were going so smoothly that the brothers feared moving back into a permanent building.

Some loyal customers insisted that the tent was fun and made for a great ambience. But the decision was made for them in 2014.

One afternoon, while customers were dining and Amrik Singh was overseeing the service, he saw a spark from one of the electrical wires on the ceiling of the tent. Before he could do anything, the roof caught fire. The customers hurriedly ran out. And before the fire brigade showed up, it had all turned to dust. The brothers and the staff cleared the rubble, laid out the tables again, and were serving dinner within a few hours. Amrik Singh saw humour in the situation. Customers who had seen the fire had moved on, and the ones who were just walking in had no idea that the dhaba had been ablaze a while back. This diehard commitment to keeping the kitchen running is a defining feature of Amrik Sukhdev's legacy.

The new building was thrown open to the public on 7 January 2014.

The next decade would bring its own challenges, but Amrik Sukhdev would never struggle the way it had before. It would stop being a dhaba and evolve into something new. Some things would remain constant amidst all the changes. For example, the stress on clean bathrooms; they would double the restroom capacity in 2018. But the part that would see most changes was the menu.

The Food, the Name

Ayandrali Dutta, editor at *HT Slurrp*, remembers her first visit to Amrik Sukhdev more than two decades ago, in 2003, like it was just yesterday. Coming from a small city, the midnight rush was quite the sight for her. It continues to be a midnight hangout spot, and she is always amazed by the rows of cars parked there at all hours.

'I still can't forget how the magnificent dinner we had—dal, roti, stuffed paratha loaded with white butter, and rice—was served on charpais. The steaming fluffy parathas with homemade butter and chai continue to reign supreme for me,' she says.

I asked Amrik Singh and Suraj Singh if they still consider parathas to be their main offering. As an answer to my question, Amrik Singh reflected on how the dhaba signifies a variety of experiences for its diverse groups of diners. To those who travel on the highway, it is a dhaba. For the people of the Sonipat town, it is a restaurant. It is this transformation that their menu reflects. Amrik Sukhdev currently boasts a massive Indian sweets section and a full-fledged bakery. While it may seem that the brand is losing focus, for the founding family, the spotlight continues to remain on fulfilling the needs of the customer, no matter how much they change.

The children of NRIs who visited India at the turn of the century demanded pizzas and burgers. Some others wanted Chinese. The families who lived nearby wanted chaat and snacks. Not all additions were made by customer demand though. One winter, they procured gajar ka halwa from a shop in town, and it sold out within hours. The demand kept increasing until they began acquiring the entire production of the shop. Then one day, a sweet maker walked in, looking for a job. Amrik Singh threw him a challenge. If he could match the finesse of the halwa, he could have the job. The sweet maker passed the test and slowly took over the kitchen. First, he made rasgullas, and then went on to make different sweets during his free time. The menu expanded as did the desserts team.

This organic growth is quite different from the strategy and long-term vision-led growth that we see in corporate brands. I asked Suraj Singh about his plans as the heir of Amrik Sukhdev. He confesses that he does not have a vision yet. But he speaks of the hotel we are sitting in—Home In. This posh hotel started operating in 2017, the year he got married. The hotel was nearing completion at the time of his marriage. He joked that his wedding was the occasion for the hotel's soft launch and visiting relatives were its first guests. There had been a few rooms earlier which were rented out to tired travellers at a nominal sum. But today, the swanky hotel is a business in its own right and caters to the town and multiple universities nearby.

You may have noticed that we have not yet spoken of how Amrik Sukhdev got its name. That is an incident that summarizes the decision-making process at play here. It is hard to imagine that the establishment did not have a name till 1985. One day, Prakash's sons, Amrik Singh and Sukhdev Singh, went up to their father and reasoned that the growing business needed a name. Prakash Singh replied, 'Naam toh upar wale ka hota hai (All name and fame belongs to the Almighty)'. He did not want to name his creation; he considered it arrogant. Yet he finally relented and agreed to a brand name, coining it by combining the names of his two sons—Amrik Sukhdev.

As we talked about the changing menu, I asked if they remembered when tawa parathas had first made an appearance. For a few years, they had been available; then suddenly they were taken off the menu. Amrik Singh recollected why parathas started being made in the tandoor, but he does not remember when the shift happened. As the number of tables increased, it became difficult to churn out tawa parathas to meet the increasing demand. The tandoor was easier and faster. My question got Suraj Singh curious, and he is now researching to find out more about the shift and when it happened.

Fortunately, the tawa parathas had been off the menu for so long that bringing them back as a retro curiosity made sense, and Amrik Singh had done just that a few months ago. He wanted us to try them. Within fifteen minutes, a platter was brought in with the parathas, dal, curd, white butter, and pickles. The parathas were crisp, generously stuffed, and much less doughy than their tandoori counterparts. Curiously, Amrik Singh forbade me from putting any butter on the paratha. He said it would ruin them. He was right, of course, but it is remarkable how parathas with a huge serving of white butter have become a trademark of both Murthal and Amrik Sukhdev.

The dal at Amrik Sukhdev is the second longest-running item on the menu. Interestingly, the earlier version of the dal was always kept light because it accompanied the heavy parathas. It did not have too much tempering, butter, or cream—unlike what is served in the dhaba these days. Amrik Singh tried bringing back the former, simpler dal, but customers complained, and the rich, butter-laden dal prevailed.

The dal on my plate was the older type, served without any tempering, and it stood out for its rustic and simple flavours. Then I had a plate of their famed kulchas which I sincerely believe is made for award shortlists. The kulcha was different from the spongy bread that you get on the streets of Delhi. This one was crispy and crumbly like a puff pastry minus the puff. The chole, again, was distinct from its darker Delhi counterpart. This one was mildly spiced, slightly sweet, and the gravy was the colour of a tomato.

Once the food was served, it became difficult to

resume the conversation. I still had many questions, but as I asked one, Amrik Singh would call over a server and order something else. I did manage to ask them about dhabas, where they thought the concept was headed, and if they saw a role for themselves as a brand that has spearheaded the concept for so many decades.

Here the father and the son had slightly different takes. The father thought the dhabas as they used to be were not practical any more. Customers want hygienic dhabas, uniformed staff, bottled water, clean washrooms, and no mosquitoes—that is the very definition of a restaurant. The son believes dhabas have been inspiring restaurants; for instance, the open and live kitchen idea in high-end restaurants is one such takeaway. A bowl of kheer interrupted us. The kheer first appeared on the menu in the early 1980s, the same time as paneer parathas.

For customers, however, Amrik Sukhdev continues to be the very definition of a dhaba. But as the brand transforms, so does the dining experience of those who expect an old-school dhaba. Dinesh Rathi, who works at a technology startup, notes, 'Having moved from Maharashtra, the idea of a dhaba in terms of scale and ambience was very different. I was expecting a very basic set-up. However, when I got there, I was amazed at its scale. It practically is a restaurant—the word dhaba probably stuck for legacy reasons.'

Anurag Khaund, a student pursuing doctoral studies

in international relations in Gujarat, still remembers his first dining experience in Amrit Sukhdev in 2011, 'when it was still a small shack and had not yet developed into the concrete structure it is today.' Originally from Assam, his first trip to North India had to include a halt at Amrik Sukhdev.

'I remember having stopped there for breakfast on our journey to Amritsar. It was the first dhaba that gave me an experience of the mouthwatering paratha with desi butter. I remember my stomach being full after just two pieces of the giant parathas. Now, whenever I order parathas at any other restaurant, I measure them against the Amrik Sukhdev ones.'

Amrik Sukhdev continues to mean many different things to different people. As Amrik Singh said, the times are changing and dhabas will change too. The shacks may go and new concrete buildings may come up in their place. But their bathrooms will remain clean. The midnight stops will be safe and abuzz with people. There will always be piping hot parathas, melting white butter, and hot cups of tea waiting for every tired driver who drives past Murthal. Once you think of the sheer number of lives the establishment has touched over the seven decades and how it continues to draw thousands every day, it is not a surprise that they were recognized as legendary by Taste Atlas.

Must-have Dishes at Amrik Sukhdev Dhaba

Aloo pyaaz paratha

Parathas are flatbreads that are stuffed with different ingredients and then cooked on a tawa or baked in a tandoor. They can be soft, crispy, and flaky, all at the same time. Though the choice of stuffing ranges from potatoes, onions, paneer (cottage cheese), and cauliflowers, the combination of onions and potatoes is the crowd favourite at Amrik Sukhdev Dhaba. They are always served piping hot with a side of curd and pickles. You can combine it with dal or curry if you wish, but it is not required. If you are accustomed to the tandoor ones, try the tawa parathas.

Amritsari chole and kulcha

Kulcha is a leavened Indian bread, unlike parathas that contain no yeast or yoghurt or soda. Kulchas are made of all-purpose flour, again unlike the parathas, which are made with whole wheat flour. The kulchas at Amrik Sukhdev are unlike the pillowy ones that you find in Delhi, but they are very close to the flaky ones popular in Amritsar. The accompanying chole, in a reddish creamy gravy, is low on spices. It goes amazingly well with the kulcha, achieving a perfect balance.

Amritsari dal

The famed dal of Amrik Sukhdev is a mix of urad (split black lentils) and rajma (kidney beans). Slow cooked to perfection, these lentils are soft but they never fully disintegrate. Even without the richness of added cream and butter, this dish tastes of wholesome goodness. They call it dal makhani because that is what most people understand a good dal to be, but this dal is much more rustic and a perfect accompaniment to rich parathas.

Makkhan

Makkhan or white butter has a legendary status on the Punjabi platter. This unprocessed and fresh local butter has no added salt or preservatives. It is the butter that is made at homes and still has much nostalgia attached to it. It tastes lighter and more of milk than the yellow packaged versions. The parathas are accompanied by a bowl of makkhan, and you can buy a pack if you want.

Kheer

Kheer is a pudding that has three base ingredients—rice, milk, and sugar. It can have a wide variety of garnishes and enrichments, but many a times, the best ones are also the simplest. The kheer at Amrik Sukhdev is exactly that; it is the base elements that shine through. It is milky, not too sweet, and you can finish a bowl all by yourself.

A FAMILY'S COMMITMENT TO CONSISTENCY

Mavalli Tiffin Rooms (MTR), Bengaluru (32)

Ruth Dsouza Prabhu

I often discuss what I am working on with my mother who takes a keen interest in all of my food-related work. After all, she is a cookbook author herself. I was talking to her about the piece I was writing on Mavalli Tiffin Rooms (MTR) in Bengaluru. My father, who is usually a silent listener on our phone calls (my mother loves the speaker button), piped up saying, 'I used to go there when I was studying at RV Engineering College!'

Dad, all of seventy-five in 2023, went back in time to 1967–68. 'I was living at the St Joseph's hostel which was near Lalbagh, if memory serves right. On weekends, my engineering classmates and I would walk across to MTR for breakfast. Masala dosas and filter coffee were the standard order. My personal favourite those days was the masala dosa—crisp and well roasted with the potato bhaji on the inside. The coconut chutney and sambar that were served with it made it even better,' he said. At the end of this conversation, I realized that all through my childhood, Dad's standard order when we ordered breakfast was a masala dosa—perhaps the one he used to enjoy at MTR triggered a lifelong love for the dish, even if he never finished that engineering degree.

I remember my first visit to MTR very clearly. Around twenty years ago, working as a full-time media professional, I would bulk cook on the weekends and freeze those meals for use during the week. Back then, I was newly married and still learning my way around the kitchen.

One Sunday, my husband and I decided to catch an early morning screening of the Hrithik Roshan starrer *Lakshya* (2004). I hurriedly wrapped up my cooking, turning off the pressure cooker as I rushed out of the door. Three hours later, we came home, and as we opened the door, the most horrid smell of burnt metal smacked us in the face. Instead of turning off the fire, I had set it on simmer! Not only had my dish burnt beyond recognition, my cooker had too. I was inconsolable till my husband took me to MTR for their vegetarian meal. That steady stream of around twenty dishes that were served at a rhythmic pace made me feel better. Their Sunday special—a sweet called chandrahara—topped off the meal. We were satiated and smiled all the way home for a much-needed siesta. The blackened cooker was soon replaced.

Just like for my father and I, MTR over the decades has been at the centre of thousands of memories. And to go back in time and hear its story, I met with fifty-two-year-old Hemamalini Maiya, the third-generation owner of MTR, at the Bowring Institute in Bengaluru, one cloudy Friday evening. Hemamalini (fondly called Mala) and I had met a few times before as judges on a restaurant award panel. We share a friendly rapport, which made the almost three-and-a-half-hour chat a free-flowing one.

From Farmlands to Kitchens

'Our family comes from humble beginnings; we belong to Parampalli village in Saligrama town of the Udupi/Dakshina Kannada (DK) district. My grandfather and four grand-uncles were all farmers. But, farming was a hard life; getting money and food was difficult. Proficient at cooking, the brothers decided to come to Bangalore to seek their fortunes as cooks in people's homes. They arrived here in 1920, my grandfather staying back to look after the farmlands,' Hemamalini tells me.

Parameshwara Maiya and Ganappayya Maiya secured employment as cooks in the homes of some of the most prominent people of Bangalore. Four years later, in 1924, Parameshwara, who was working for a court judge, was encouraged and bankrolled by his employer to start a small restaurant of his own. He started this venture with Ganappayya, naming the establishment Brahmin Coffee Club. Situated at Lalbagh Fort Road (perpendicular to today's Lalbagh Road), idlis and coffee were the mainstay there.

'It was a small eatery, but it made a name for itself. Because of the lack of space, they offered car service. People would drive up and be served in their cars.' That's all Hemamalini knows about the Brahmin Coffee Club.

Parameshwara Maiya passed away just five years later, leaving Ganappayya to manage things alone. To help him, their youngest brother, Yagnanarayana Maiya, joined the business.

Between the two brothers, it was Yagnanarayana, fondly called Yagnappa, who was the most passionate and imaginative when it came to food. 'Every recipe we have today is all thanks to his creativity and invention. He was the front of MTR, and every photograph you see has him in it. Ganappayya took care of all the backend processes including the accounting,' Hemamalini tells me.

Passing on the MTR Mantle through Generations

Yagnappa was a showman and knew how to read his audience. 'The family always had plenty of stories to share about my uncle,' says Hemamalini. 'It was a joint family of eleven brothers (including cousins) and their children. They were all educated—doctors, engineers, and scientists, and Yagnappa was the youngest. After he took over the restaurant, he managed it effortlessly, working in enterprising ways to build the brand and win it fame and recognition. The popularity that MTR enjoys today has to be attributed to everything he did.'

One such undertaking was a Europe tour he went on in 1951 to understand how restaurants in that part of the world functioned. He returned an informed man, highly impressed by the protocols the eateries had in place to ensure cleanliness and discipline. He introduced several changes to the way the restaurant functioned, raising the standards of hygiene and sanitation.

Brahmin Coffee Club moved to its current location in 1960, and Yagnappa renamed it Mavalli Tiffin Rooms, a doff of the hat to the location they were in. There are two buildings here today. The original one houses the restaurant, and the second one adjoining it was bought several years later and converted into the shop that one sees today. At the restaurant, Yagnappa introduced the sterilization of all utensils, crockery, and cutlery. He opened the kitchen to diners who wanted to see how their food was being cooked. The scrutiny, he believed, would keep the staff on their toes. Interesting, considering that the hallmark of many Udupi restaurants that opened in Mumbai from the 1930s onwards was such open kitchens.

He even put together a booklet of dos and don'ts of dining etiquette, some points being quite humorous: 'Don't put curry leaves from your food on the table—put them on the plate'; 'Don't brush your hair in the dining hall'. This immediately took me back. While not at MTR, this second rule was the reason I was once admonished at the Ideal Ice Cream outlet in Mangaluru (another legacy establishment). However, in that case, I was just retying my ponytail and not brushing my hair! The logic of it makes perfect sense to me though.

Around 1964, Yagnappa was diagnosed with cancer. Before his untimely death in Parampalli, he wanted to make sure that someone took over MTR from him. At that time, women were not encouraged to be a part of the business. Hemamalini's uncle (her father's elder brother) was a scientist and had left for the USA. Yagnappa's son, Sadanand Maiya, was still studying and was too young to take on the responsibility. So Yagnappa zeroed in on his nephew, Harishchandra Maiya, Hemamalini's father.

'My father came into the business as a young boy. While studying in Bangalore (he had done a double degree—Bachelor in Arts and Commerce), he would spend time working at MTR, at the cash counter as well as doing other things (as did all his siblings through the years; however, they all went on to other careers while Harishchandra remained). Yagnappa felt that my father was best suited to carry MTR's legacy forward. This was perhaps taking into consideration that he had a lot of similar traits as my grand-uncle and had imbibed a lot of his (Yagnappa's) ways of running the show in his own approach to the job,' Hemamalini says.

However, Harishchandra was not initially interested in taking over MTR, and he went to Bombay to pursue another passion—music. Her father was an ardent music lover and had a massive collection recalls Hemamalini. She remembers getting ready for school with classical music playing in the background at home. Her mother told her that her father (Harishchandra) went to Bombay to see if he could do something in the field of music. But he was soon brought back to MTR to take over the reins.

Harishchandra eventually took over MTR from Yagnappa who passed away in 1968 at the age of sixty-two. Just like Yagnappa, Harishchandra was a stickler about how every dish should taste. He wouldn't hesitate to wash a plate if needed. 'They all grew up doing every job in the restaurant, and there was complete dignity of labour. That was my grand-uncle's legacy, and he treated his employees as equals,' Hemamalini explains. Every day, her family would sit with all the employees for staff meals. 'There were around thirty people in those days, and we would be served with them. They each had their own tumblers, with their names engraved on them, if I remember right.'

Harishchandra continued to build the legacy of MTR through the turbulent seventies, then the eighties and nineties. However, in 1999, soon after he turned sixty-two, he passed away. Hemamalini, then the oldest in the family at twenty-seven, was clearly next in line, her brothers being too young to step in. A day after her father's passing, she walked into MTR, flanked by her two uncles for moral support. Women had thus far never steered MTR. This was going to be a first, for everyone.

The Story of MTR's Food

It was going to be quite a journey for Hemamalini and MTR at the turn of the century. But before that, let me go back to tell you the story of MTR's food—the cornerstone of its legacy.

Today, MTR has nine outlets in Bengaluru, including the flagship restaurant at Lalbagh. They also have branches in Mysore, Udupi, and one on the Hassan highway. Internationally, they have franchisee outlets in Singapore, Dubai, London, and Kuala Lumpur. In Bengaluru, breakfast, lunch, and dinner are served at all outlets, with the exception of the one in Lalbagh which does not serve dinner.

One would assume that the food here would be representative of the family's roots in Parampalli and Saligrama. On the contrary, Hemamalini tells me, the food is most likely a blend of the Mysore and the DK regions. This is owing to the geographical and political lines that existed when the restaurant was first started. Alongside Yagnappa's unique touch, it was the masalas that gave the food at MTR its distinct taste.

Take MTR's sambar and rasam. Both are typically from DK, with sweeter undertones. The khara bath (a vegetable dish made with semolina, diced vegetables, and spices and usually served for breakfast) is not a typical DK dish, but the masalas that have gone into it have created a uniquely MTR version. 'You can't slot our food into any specific cuisine,' says Hemamalini. The bisi bele bath (a porridge-like mix of rice, lentils, and vegetables with a spice mix and tamarind base and finished with a ghee tempering) is a dish from the Mysore region. Yagnappa took the original one and made it richer by adding in a special masala blend, sambar onions, cashew nuts, and plenty of ghee. In fact, the primary medium of cooking at MTR is ghee—something the brand takes a great deal of pride in. And we definitely love ghee in everything!

While I have had numerous breakfasts at MTR, writing this essay was the perfect excuse for another one. I compared notes with my father and realized that the experience is by and large the same. Walking up the few concrete steps to MTR's double door is like crossing the threshold into another period. Along the wall to your right is a bench for those waiting their turn. Over the bench are the many framed awards that MTR has been bestowed with over the years.

The cashier at the counter signals us, in the middle of his many ongoing transactions, to make our way upstairs to be seated. On the way, you see wooden panels of framed black and white photographs of famous personalities who have dined at MTR and of events the restaurant has catered. These frames are all over the many dining rooms across the upper floor of the restaurant. If you end up in the waiting area at the top of the staircase, there are large frames displaying multiple photographs—like one of the tenth anniversary of the Chamber of Commerce, Bangalore City, that MTR catered on 19 December 1946.

Once seated on the signature red plastic chairs, you either know what you want to order or you ask for the day's menu. It will be recited, beginning with their popular dishes, and if you still haven't ordered through the recital, then the rest of the menu. For breakfast that day, we started with the kesari bath. The version here is a mix of both semolina and vermicelli and is not cloyingly sweet. Studded with raisins and made in generous amounts of ghee, it sets the right tone for the rest of the meal. Next up was the rava idli, a MTR creation that harks back to World War II and speaks to Yagnappa's ingenuity. Idlis, which are a highlight of their menu, are made from rice. However, during World War II, Japan invaded Burma, the largest producer of rice in the region and the chief supplier to South India. Naturally, this caused a shortage, and MTR was among the many affected eateries.

Yagnappa experimented with rava (semolina), soaking it in curd, mixing in curry leaves and coriander, giving it a tempering of mustard seeds and cashew nuts in ghee, and then steaming it as one would a regular idli. The result was a fluffy, lighter idli that people couldn't get enough of long after the war was over. On our table that day, it came with a small steel container of molten ghee to pour over it and some chutney and sagu (a vegetable curry).

Those were not his only innovations. After his Europe sojourn, Yagnappa created the chandrahara. This pastry-like dessert consists of layers of flour that are deep-fried to a biscuity goodness and then topped with a sweet, thick sauce made from khoya. Available only on Sundays, this sweet was initially called 'French sweet', but it didn't catch the interest of diners. That was until Yagnappa renamed it chandrahara after a hit film that was playing at a theatre nearby. People couldn't get enough of it. I tried looking up this movie, and while I didn't find a *Chandrahara* from that time there was N. T. Rama Rao's *Chandraharam* released in 1954.

Yagnappa also came up with the French fruit mixture with American ice cream, a dish which is still served. 'We have no clue why he called it that, but this Europe trip must have been inspiring,' Hemamalini tells me, pointing out that even the word tiffin in the establishment's name was a British term. 'He did things his own way, and people took to it because it was so different,' she adds.

'In my grand-uncle's time, once the restaurant closed for the day around 7.30 p.m., we had dinner parties for around 100 people. These took place about three times a week,' she tells me, adding that these were forty-course dinners with seven types of sweets, appetizers, and main courses. And the amazing part? It was a sit-down service!

Coming back to our breakfast, two dosas came to the table. One was the pudi dosa—a thick open dosa with a blob of potato bhaji in its centre and smeared generously with pudi (powdered lentils and chilli that is added over a dosa with a layer of ghee to help spread it). The other was the classic MTR masala dosa—a well-roasted triangle which hides the bhaji. Both are served with a little container of ghee on the side. Accompaniments of chutney and sambar completed the dishes, and there was silence at the table till we were done eating. A filter coffee that is finished with some frothy milk foam on top signalled the end of breakfast.

Their filter coffee played a huge role in MTR's legacy. It was a beverage that spurred conversations among freedom fighters, businessmen, and more. Yagnappa's dedication to perfecting the brew was unparalleled. He would painstakingly select, roast, and grind beans every day to ensure he achieved the flavour he wanted. He used buffalo milk to enhance the taste. Back then, the coffee was served in silver cups with a precise quarter inch of froth on top. That froth we were sipping truly had a story behind it, and Hemamalini recounted how the family worked hard on preserving the integrity of their coffee.

In 1976, during the Emergency, restaurants across the country were asked to reduce prices to match those approved by the government. For Harishchandra, this was not a feasible proposition because there was no way he was going to compromise on quality of the food. So, while he sold a dosa at ₹1.25, i.e. for half its original price, he did not cut corners in any way. What they did not anticipate was the surge in the number of patrons. Their losses mounted, and each day the restaurant displayed a board outside stating these figures. Soon, in 1976, they decided to shut the doors to the restaurant. Instead, the upper floor where we had our breakfast was converted into a space where they began making masalas and mixes for rava idli and khara bath, an initiative undertaken to help support their staff. Since they were already making them for the restaurant, it was easy enough to package and sell these. That was the beginning of MTR's packaged food business which went on to become hugely popular. Fortunately, their closure at the peak of the Emergency lasted for only a few months, and soon the restaurant resumed its operations. 'The shop became one of those first superstores,' says Hemamalini. 'Today's outlet is a much smaller version. All this happened next to the restaurant. In 1991, operations moved to a factory in Bommasandra and the masala-making area was converted into a dining space.'

In 1997, Harishchandra started lunch and dinner services. It was a twenty-five-course meal. 'This lavish meal was priced back then at ₹50, and we would serve around a thousand lunches in three hours. It was an exhausted workforce we had those days,' reminisces Hemamalini.

For around two to three months, the thalis used were specially created silver ones. They had 400 of these made along with silver spoons. But people decided to help themselves to the cutlery and crockery. Also, the plates weighed close to a kilogram each and carrying a stack of them for washing up and down flights of stairs was a strain. Their use was eventually stopped. Even today there are diners who remember the silver plates and ask about them.

The silver plates turned to steel plates, but the restaurant continued to serve its signature grape juice in silver tumblers, till eventually, they had to stop that too thanks to sticky fingers. The menu was trimmed down some more, considering the wastage that was taking place. Today, it comprises around fifteen to twenty items, including condiments.

And soon enough, to experience the brilliance of that meal, we found ourselves at MTR for lunch. After paying and getting our coupons at the cashier's, we headed upstairs where a member of the staff checked them off as ready-to-be-seated. He even confirmed if everyone in our party of two had arrived. We were led down several narrow corridors, doors lining them, opening out into small dining rooms filled to capacity.

We were seated in a small room that had just two tables with four seats each. Instantly, there appeared the segmented steel thali, a tumbler for water, and one with chilled grape juice. In quick succession, our plate was filled with shavige (vermicelli) payasam, a vegetable sagu, sprouts, moong kosambari (a salad), and a coconut chutney. Few minutes later came a large tray of crispy, roasted mini masala dosas which had us blowing on our fingers as we broke into the hot surfaces. Next up, gojju ambade (an urad dal vada dunked in coconut gravy), a ghee-laden helping of bisi bele bath (there were enough cashews to make one smile) with raita, and mini papads on the side. Soon after came the vangi bath (brinjal rice), followed in quick succession by white rice, sambar, rasam, and a helping of curd rice. For dessert, we were served fruit salad with ice cream.

This was a lot of food, but what stood out distinctly was the wonderfully different and unique flavors present in each dish. The core ingredient comes shining through, and nothing feels like it was made in a hurry to feed the hordes. The pace is just leisurely enough to allow you to enjoy it; you are asked if you would like seconds and thirds, leaving you sated and happy.

Hemamalini's father's cousin, today their general manager, is the custodian of all of MTR's recipes. He manages all the outlets and the restaurant managers report to him. He began his career as a server, growing to become the cashier. It was Harishchandra who noticed all that hidden potential and put it to work.

Which brings me back Hemamalini's story.

A Change of Guard

'I remember that first walk into MTR, with my two uncles beside me. Everyone was looking at me. I didn't know what to expect. My mother was initially quite against me getting into the business, but I said I have to do this for my father—it was a very emotional decision. Our regular customers were having coffee and turned around to look at me. They didn't know I was coming to take over. Dad had passed away suddenly and had not groomed anybody to take over from him, though he did try explaining things to me towards the end.' Hemamalini tells me.

She had no experience whatsoever in the operations of the restaurant and worked on pure instinct: 'I knew what had to be done. The resistance would come around two years later. Till then people at the restaurant knew that if the place had to run, I would be the one to run it. Resistance came in the form of insolence, people simply trying to push their luck to see how far they could take things.'

Hemamalini narrates one of many incidents she distinctly remembers.

'It was about our dosas. They were just not coming out right. When I entered the dosa-making area, I told the team that both the colour and quality of the dosas were not up to the mark. The head dosa-maker answered, "Neene bandh madu (You make it)", addressing me in the singular. I was livid. How dare you, I asked, and told him to leave, adding that it was my kitchen, and if necessary, I would call others to remove him. My manager at that time, a second cousin, was an old-timer. He tried to convince me to let things be. However, I insisted that allowing such behaviour would only open the door to more disrespect. The man continued to protest loudly, and I physically blocked his entry into the restaurant. I made it clear that the more he acted out, the more convinced I was of my decision to remove him.

'His raving and ranting went on for a few hours. I went upstairs, and I sat there, while he continued [ranting] outside. I warned everybody that no one was to allow him in. It was such a spectacle! Our customers came to warn me to not go outside while he was there. He finally realized nothing was going to work and approached Ganesh, our current manager and then cashier, asking him to put in a word with me to help fix the situation. That night he came and fell at my feet. Everybody had left by then. I asked: "Why are you falling at my feet? If at all, you should ask my father for forgiveness because you have insulted the organization and not me." My father had once helped this man through a health scare. Letting him go was a call I had to take and a precedent I had to set.'

Today, Hemamalini feels she would probably not deal with such a situation the same way. But in those days, she had no choice but to show that side of her. The MTR factory had a union and that found its way to the restaurant, both bodies founded by the same person.

Hemamalini spent days in the labour commissioner's office, negotiating terms. 'There was the constant threat of a strike call. Finally, I had enough and refused to budge. I told the union president that they could go on strike, and we would all take a much-needed holiday. It was after this that my younger brother Arvind stepped in to handle all matters related to human resources. I don't interfere in it at all.' She looks quite relieved that those stressful days are behind her.

After the union problem was resolved, things started to fall into place. 'We can scream from the rooftops about gender equality but, on the ground, we have to accept the reality of the situation,' observes Hemamalini. 'Once my brothers joined full time, there was a change because there were now men in the business. They would listen to my brothers. I had had to fight much harder. Arvind is much like my father. He takes hard decisions and doesn't waver.'

Bringing in the New

MTR's expansion began with the outlet in Rajajinagar—a hesitant experiment by Hemamalini and her team. 'Our advisor, out for his daily bonda (tender coconut), spotted a building and called me asking if I would be interested in starting an MTR there. It was a sari showroom. We began in 2004, and it ran till 2014–15. There were several issues with the place, but it gave us an insight into how we would function if we were outside of the main MTR. We realized that even the water we use matters,' she says.

When it comes to the coffee, there will always be a slight change in flavour at each outlet. 'To standardize this, coffee is now made with RO water in all branches. But initially, we brought water from Lalbagh to the Rajajinagar outlet for a while. At Lalbagh, the coffee will always retain a unique flavour because the rate at which it is consumed here is so high that the decoction moves at record speed.'

In 2007, the brand opened four outlets, each within a month of the other at Whitefield, Gandhinagar, JP Nagar, and St Mark's Road. 'It was the first set of our restaurants coming up, and there was a lot of learning. We would train chefs from A to Z—Ganesh and I were in charge of quality control,' she recalls. Centralization of masalas used was also necessary to ensure the consistency of the dishes. 'Everything is about the roasting of the masalas, and we figured that at the hands of different cooks, everything changes. So now we make masalas centrally, and these mixes are sent to all our branches. A cook simply has to follow the recipes with the masalas made. He doesn't have to learn how to make them. We began this around a decade ago.'

With all the franchisee outlets that MTR opened, the one thing Hemamalini decided against was diversifying the menu to attract more people to the restaurants: 'Our franchisees did ask us if they could, but our motto is to do what you are good at and stick to it. It may take some time for people to understand our cuisine, to like and love it, but if we stick to it, we will get the crowd. So no other cuisines are allowed.'

At the moment, the family has put a pause on domestic expansion because they want to stabilize their existing outlets and plans. 'It's a constant effort and requires all of us to put our heads together. Employee crunch is what all restaurants—especially at the kitchen staff level—face. But, we are looking at international expansion. We have just opened a branch in Seattle, USA, in December 2023. And then Kathmandu in Nepal is on the cards too,' says Hemamalini.

Attrition is an issue they deal with. 'Employees in the 80s and 90s would stay. Today's employees, not so much. We do have those who have been in the kitchen for over a decade, but it is with the cleaning and serving staff where we see high attrition. Currently, the brand has 600 employees, not counting franchisee outlets,' she explains.

In 2024, MTR will turn 100, and today, Hemamalini wouldn't mind involving professionals from outside the family in the business. In her opinion, new blood and newer ideas will become important if they look at further expansion in the future. At this moment, their bandwidth remains stretched. Nonetheless, she is certain that the Lalbagh restaurant will remain unchanged—it will be the family that will run things. 'There is so much history on the walls there, that I think it's something to be proud of, to preserve and carry on....'

Must-have Dishes at Mavalli Tiffin Rooms

Chandrahara

This iconic sweet is available only on Sundays at MTR and is much loved. These little deep-fried triangles of refined flour and semolina are held together with a single clove. Over them is poured a reduced and sweetened milk concoction laden with saffron and dry fruit that makes every bite an indulgent treat. Well worth the wait.

Bisi bele bath

This is a hearty breakfast dish that takes the standard sambar rice mix a step further. A soft, rich mash of rice and lentils made with a signature spice mix, the bisi bele bath is finished with a tempering of cashew nuts in ghee, making each hot bite an absolute delight.

Rava idli

Considering this dish was invented at MTR, you can't possibly miss savouring its pillowy goodness with a side of chutney. Airy and light, much like a dhokla shaped like an idli, the rava idli here is studded with broken bits of cashew, curry leaves, and mustard seeds that add to its flavour.

Vegetarian meals

Go prepared! Close to twenty dishes come to your plate in synchronized succession, and you can ask for repeats. The meal begins with two kinds of sweets, goes into flavoured rice, puris with seasonal vegetable dishes, rice, sambar, rasam, and a few more sweets to close the deal. What you absolutely should not miss—the cold pulpy fresh grape juice that comes with the meal.

Filter coffee

Every sip of this coffee is a reminder of how its consistency has been built along with that of the restaurant. The frothy milk on top adds to the experience and is a signature.

A CUISINE, A CENTURY, A LEGEND

Karim's, New Delhi (84)

OM ROUTRAY

History is as much a product of academic research as it is of popular and collective remembrance, and for a city like New Delhi that has a living memory of a few centuries and an archaeological history that goes back thousands of years, 1913 is modern history.

Delhi was just two years into being the capital of British India, the Delhi Durbar of 1911 having culminated in the transfer of the seat of power from Calcutta. The city was still getting used to the idea of being a capital. The foundations for New Delhi had been laid. The Viceroy's House, today the Rashtrapati Bhawan, was already under construction. The famed architect of the British Raj, Edwin Lutyens, was busy sketching new buildings and planning wide avenues. King George V and Queen Mary had left but the colonial government was slowly gathering mass. In those initial years, one definite outcome that emerged out of the establishment of New Delhi was that the once livelier part of the city became 'Old' Delhi. But the bylanes were not as narrow nor were the streets congested yet, the way they are today.

That said, this part of Delhi was never far from the bustle, and one can certainly assume Karim's was not the first food establishment in that neighbourhood. In 1913, Delhi resident Haji Karimuddin must have been a cautious but hopeful entrepreneur.

Looking back from 2023, it is hard to ascertain what could have come before Karim's and then stood the test of time. The closest perhaps is Moti Mahal, that started off in Peshawar in 1920, and after Partition, opened shop 930 kilometres away in Daryaganj in 1947. There is Wenger's in Connaught Place, established in 1924. Kake-Da-Hotel opened in 1931. Britannia & Co. in Mumbai in 1923, completing a hundred years in 2023. Most of Kolkata's vintage eateries came much later too. Does that make Karim's the longest running restaurant in the country? It might just.

A Cart Full of Hope

Today, Karim's is an epic tale of evolving to stay the same. There are branches and franchises, and the brand is more visible than ever before. So it's a wonder how the restaurant has not just survived but has thrived for over a century. Few realize the complexities the brand must have faced as the leading ambassador of Mughlai cuisine. Behind the scenes, massive efforts are being made to keep the food experience exactly the way it was.

With this context and a thousand questions in my mind, I went to meet the family that presently runs Karim's. The meeting was scheduled at the original outlet in Old Delhi. I have been coming here since my college days at Delhi University, twenty years ago. Back then, we were a hungry lot but did not have much money. So, we ate at small street eateries. We would pool our money, around ₹150 to ₹200 each, to indulge in a meal of mutton seekh kababs. It was our biggest food bill for the month. Once we all began working, and I started eating out a lot more, Karim's remained that one immensely affordable place. Especially when you consider that you are dining at an institution of such heritage.

Stepping back into Old Delhi, what has not changed much are the lanes. Karim's is just 50 metres or so from gate one of Jama Masjid, yet you have to drive past it and into the heart of Old Delhi to find parking. I have accompanied many friends who drive right up to the gate and try their luck. I prefer to park in front of Prince Paan on the main road, cross over to the Moti Mahal side, and then hail a rickshaw. These days, there are fewer hand-pulled rickshaws and more of the battery-operated ones. The ride is short, but something I still have to steel myself for.

The lane leading to the Jama Masjid from the main road is the sort of experience that global tourists imagine when they come to India. A sea of people flowing violently through a narrow channel. You do not navigate these waters, you just let it move you. Cars, bikes, rickshaws, carts loaded with goods, cycles loaded with wares, pedestrians trying to dodge everything, adolescents on horses, load-bearing donkeys, and people in queues at eateries or coming out of shops—the street leading to Karim's gives you a sense of Old Delhi unlike any other experience.

If you manage to look up from the back of the rickshaw, you catch the first sight of the imposing Jama Masjid—the minarets, the walls that mimic a fort's, and the giant dome rising above Meena Bazaar on your right. These days, surrounded by that free-flowing crowd, you will fear phone snatching and think twice, but will still end up pulling it out for a photograph. It is right there at the stairs leading up to gate number one, where Haji Karimuddin first set up a cart in 1911. This was two years before opening the Karim's that we see today. You can almost imagine it as it would have been—the masjid in the background and the cart with steaming gravies and hot rotis in front of it.

Gali Kababiyan

Karim's is ensconced in a lane christened Gali Kababiyan—the lane of kabab makers. The name came about in part thanks to another family from Bareilly who too used to make kababs here. Together, both families claim that they gave the lane the name that it still bears. However, there remains no way to substantiate this account.

From Jama Masjid gate number one, the gali is a short walk away but easy to miss. Lately, it has only become harder to spot as restaurants on both sides leading to it have bright lights, neon signs, and welcoming facades. Once you enter, the first sight of Karim's only reinforces its now seemingly obscure location.

You spot a kitchen station with large metal pots under a sign that says 'Karim Hotels Pvt Ltd. ESTD 1913'. The image is rather iconic and is plastered all over the internet. The three dining halls beyond the station are much less picturesque. Evidently, the family never hired a designer for a makeover. Keeping up with the times was not a pressure that anyone felt here. During my later conversations with the family, they kept stressing that the food has been their only ambassador. That is evident from the lack of any decor or other elements that might draw you here.

The dining areas are basic. The chairs and tables are the same as from my college years. There is always a crowd of customers waiting to be seated. Servers are carrying food from the kitchens to the tables. There is always a pile of soft, pillowy khameeri rotis on a server's platter that will catch your eye. The charcoal sigri for seekh kababs is always busy, rows of kababs being constantly turned over the fire and basted generously in oil. The rising smoke intrigues customers and one will always see a few phone cameras pointed at it.

Stepping back into the present, I was there to meet the family and was escorted through the lane beyond the dining halls. A little further on the right is the office. A monitor on the wall displays a CCTV camera feed from the restaurant and the kitchen.

Around a small table were gathered the four present directors of Karim's. Haji Karimuddin had one son, Haji Nooruddin, who in turn, had four sons: Haji Zahooruddin, Haji Sharfuddin, Haji Aleemuddin, and Haji Salahuddin. The directors are representatives of these four branches of the family. Present inside the office were Zainul Abedin (son of Zahooruddin), Jalal Uddin Akbar (son of Sharfuddin), Zaeemuddin Ahmed (son of Aleemuddin), and Saifuddin (son of Haji Salahuddin).

We began with the clarification that the restaurant that made it to Taste Atlas's list of 150 most legendary restaurants of the world was the original Karim's outlet in Gali Kababiyan. Though there are multiple branches and franchises under the brand name now, the original restaurant and Karim Hotels Pvt Ltd remain an entity separated from the others, both legally and in terms of its heritage.

In my experience, the distinctiveness of the original outlet is best experienced in its khameeri rotis and the mutton stew. Compared to the other outlets, the rotis here are thinner and crispy rather than fluffy. They are also a shade paler. The stew is much richer. After all, this is the parent outlet, steeped in the generational history and the experience of churning out such dishes. A clear difference is but a given.

During our three-hour conversation, we kept coming back to the food and the recipes. We spoke of how the family has maintained secrecy and control over the kitchen and how the needs of a growing family played a significant role in the expansion of the brand.

The Secret Remains

The secret, I was told, is that someone from the family is always present in the restaurant premises, if not in the kitchen. Eight chefs work in two shifts in the kitchen, and there are nearly sixty employees at the restaurant. The family makes sure their food is tasted every day by one of the directors before it is served. But how do they maintain quality with staff turnover? How do they make sure they are not subjected to the oscillating quality standards that all restaurants go through? How did they make sure that there are not tens of Karim's started by ex-employees?

All Karim's recipes have been trademarked. Till date, the spice mixes are prepared by the family, and the chefs are given the packets of masalas with instructions on their usage. Even if the chefs cook with the spice mixes for years, they can only guess the exact composition. The family is confident that even if the chefs prepare food elsewhere following these exact steps, without the spice mix, it will never taste the same. The balance of spices is also the secret behind the taste of their food. Every effort has been made to ensure that the culinary experience is not dependent on an individual chef's talents. There is no alternative to continuous monitoring, tasting, and being directly involved in the kitchen.

Zaeemuddin Ahmed, one of the four current directors, confirmed what I had read before. The secret spice mix is the exclusive domain of the men of the family. This is an age-old practice that one sees in different aspects of life, especially in relation to hereditary property. In this case, hereditary intellectual property. There is a fear that women, once married, may take recipes outside the family and compromise the seal of secrecy.

Enduring through the Times

We live in an era when unchanging menus can mean the death of a restaurant. But you do not go to Karim's for something new. You visit repeatedly to experience the same old taste. In fact, change in taste is the enemy of places that are built on legacy. When old timers start saying 'It's not what it used to be!', that's when trouble begins. Karim's has never had such trouble. I asked if there was a time when they struggled to attract customers or if the cuisine went out of fashion or if they remembered any instance of the business running into trouble.

After a lot of thinking by the four directors, all they could say was that business was difficult when there were riots. Another instance they could recall was during the grain shortage in 1965. Two consecutive monsoon failures caused severe droughts, and India's grain production crashed to one-fifth of its annual average. The situation was so bad that then prime minister, Lal Bahadur Shastri, appealed to the people to consume less and observe fasts. One of the cousins remembered that since wheat was not available, rotis were made with besan (gram flour). Barring these, Karim's has not seen too many lean days and there are no grand tales of struggle to keep the business afloat.

This sort of steady trajectory is a storyteller's nightmare, but every entrepreneur's envy.

'Mughlai Food Is Healthy'

When asked about their connection with the Mughal kitchens of yore, the directors say it was Mohammad Awaiz, father of the founder Haji Karimuddin, who served in the royal kitchen. During the Rebellion of 1857, he had to flee Delhi, but later returned to the city. As royalty became history, the customers of Mughlai cuisine changed. Corners were cut, and the food that was once known for its legendary richness yet subtle and delicate flavours lost its famed stature.

According to Salma Hussain, a historian specializing in Mughal dining practices, in those days, spices were few and used sparsely, reasonably, and in balance. Each dish was prepared using specific mixtures of masala, and one could not be substituted for the other. Great pains were taken for both preparing the dish as well as ensuring the final product was a visual delight.

The menu at the cart in 1911 was simple—dal, roti, and aloo gosht. Yet the family always endeavoured to bring flavours from the royal kitchens to the masses. Some recipes were passed down in the family; many others were sourced from residents of Delhi whose homes were nearby and then were perfected with their feedback.

The family firmly believes that the feeling of satisfaction that comes after a Mughlai meal is the real trademark of the cuisine. Moreover, the delicate balance of spices makes it a cuisine that is good for you, contrary to popular belief. They claim that one will never feel heavy or suffer from acidity after eating their food, a fact that my wife and I can definitely vouch for. They do make slight changes to the spice composition for winter and summer. That the consumption of spices can affect body temperature is a widely held belief in the subcontinent, and it is not surprising to find that Mughal kitchens operate on this belief too. In Urdu, certain foods are always referred to as having either a 'garam' (heat) or 'thandi' (cooling) taseer (effect) on the body.

Karim's has always been a dining destination. At the time when social media was still fresh and food lovers had just begun forming communities online, one of their first activities was to organize a dinner at Karim's. To dine at Karim's, you needed to be in large groups, or it was impossible to eat through the menu. The larger the group, the more dishes you could sample. Everyone had their favourites. For example, the famed tandoori bakra. This is a whole goat stuffed with biryani, eggs, chicken, and dry fruits and feeds fifteen people.

The family remembers the time a large French delegation had come especially to sample the bakra. Global tourists began visiting Karim's after the 1982 Asian Games. And strangely, they all ordered the same four or five dishes: murgh musallam, tandoori bakra, mutton burrah, and mutton qorma. Curious about this pattern, one of the directors asked a German tourist why they all ordered the same food from the menu. The customer pulled out a German magazine from his bag and showed him a listing for Karim's with these dishes named.

But it was not just the tourists. Eating Out in Delhi, a now defunct food group, elaborates in a blog post from November 2008 the experience of devouring a tandoori bakra. The group sent out an invitation to its members, thirty-four people showed up, and two whole roasted goats were ordered. The blog paints the table as 'a spectacle straight out of a Fred Flintstone fantasy'. The fact that group after group continued to repeat the experience says a lot about Karim's ability to unite a diverse set of people together at a table.

Typically, such tables comprise Delhiites, expats, travellers, journalists, content creators, and those who call themselves foodies. The social media landscape has transformed in the last decade, and in the world of food, Karim's continues to be a cornerstone of the capital's culinary experiences. For Delhi Food Walks, a group that conducts curated food walks for expats, tourists, and corporates, Karim's continues to be an integral part of the experience they offer in 2023, just as much as it had been when the group first began more than a decade ago in 2011 (coincidently 100 years after Haji Karimuddin set up his cart outside Jama Masjid).

It is hard to arrive at a consensus about what on Karim's menu draws more people than others. But if pressed, the list would look something like this—the dil pasand seekh kabab, or simply put, the mutton seekh kabab, would be an effortless contender for the top position. The kabab station is also one of the first sights you see upon entering Gali Kababiyan. The kabab is made from minced spiced mutton that is wrapped around a skewer and grilled on an open charcoal sigri. The skewers, the fat falling into the fire, the rising smoke, the kababi fanning the fires—modern restaurants would kill for such photogenic stations. The mutton burrah will also make the list and is my personal favourite—hunks of goat meat cooked inside a tandoor and so appropriately spiced that it pleases both lovers of mildly spiced food and those who enjoy their spices.

I have tried the lesser known dishes on the Karim's menu too. In the winter of January 2014, I tasted their lazeez saag murgh, nargisi kofte, and the shahi paneer. I remember this distinctly because I wrote about my experience on my blog. I was not a huge meat eater back then, and my post narrates how I find the mutton at Karim's easy to not just eat but to relish. The tanginess of shahi paneer catches you by surprise because when you hear the word shahi (royal), you expect a rich and sweet gravy with dry fruit paste. As someone who loves eggs in their gravy dishes, like omu rice and ros omelette, the appeal of the nargisi kofte was never lost on me. It is a boiled egg wrapped in a layer of minced meat which is then fried. The egg is then put in a thick, qorma-like gravy. The saag murgh, chicken cooked in leafy greens, is lost amidst its more famous counterparts. But it is something that must be tried to truly understand the range of the cuisine showcased by Karim's kitchens.

One dish that takes over most discussions about the food at Karim's is the kheer benazeer. The menu simply describes it as a rice pudding, completely impervious to the debate it has set off amongst food lovers. Is it a kheer or a phirni? Karim's sells this dish as kheer, but on the streets outside, something similar is sold as phirni. The difference between the two is supposed to be the integrity of the rice—whole in kheer, broken in phirni. During one of my conversations with Zaeemuddin Ahmed, I was told that phirni is supposed to be liquid, something that you can drink from a bowl. It can be made with rice or sabudana. Kheer, according to him, is not runny and can be set in earthen pots the way it is served at Karim's. I am sure the debate will continue to rage, and this is the fuel that keeps legacy brands alive. Diners, critics, writers, and reviewers pile layer upon layer of opinions, turning every legendary dish into a highly contested one as well. Karim's has no dearth of those either.

Cynthia Rosenfeld wrote in her review for the *New York Times*, '...the badam pasanda curry—a sensual combination of lamb and sweet almonds the size of figs—and finally, Karim's renowned tandoori chicken, its psychedelic sunset hue born from a slow and steady marinade.' It seems only fair that an establishment that traces its roots to the kitchens of emperor and poet Bahadur Shah Zafar is wrapped in poetry too.

India's rich, famous, and powerful have been admirers of Karim's. Bollywood actor Dilip Kumar, world renowned painter M. F. Hussain, past presidents like Fakhruddin Ali Ahmed and Zakir Hussain, as well as Indira Gandhi were all known for their love of the food there. 'Karim's had transformed from a local purveyor of aloo gosht into a monument. It was visited by princes and prime ministers, eulogized by journalists, studied by historians, and patronized by tourists,' wrote Alex Traub and Zehra Kazmi in their article for *Hindustan Times*.

At Karim's, there is rigidity regarding the recipe, but there is also flexibility in matters of the menu. I was told the story of how the paaya came to be on the menu. A qawwal who worked at All India Radio requested them to make it and offered to buy whatever was unsold.

A Legacy that Transcends Food

The food and the brand name are part of Karim's legend. But they are not the only components that made Karim's what it is. Sam Mathews, a resident of Sainik Farms in Delhi, has been a regular since the 1960s. He fondly recalls the ishtew, kababs, and sheermal. But he had an anecdote that will sum up Karim's.

'My wallet was misplaced or pickpocketed once at the crowded shahi tukda stall opposite the Karim's entrance where I had had dinner one night. I went back to Karim's to check if I misplaced it there. The senior in a spotless white kurta, with a perfectly trimmed white beard, sitting at the curry counter dishing out portions for customers told me: "Hazoor, it cannot be at Karim's or I would know. But if it is lost within the masjid area I assure you, there's no need to worry." I left. Since I was pretty lost without my cards, license, etc., I returned the next evening and met the white bearded man at the food counter. He smiled and handed me my wallet with everything intact. I smiled and kissed his hand and there was not a word exchanged. Such is the brotherhood of great men and their concern. Deeds, not words.'

Imagine a thousand such stories like this told and retold over the years. It is hard to break down success and separate the tangible from the intangible. No matter how much we write about the cuisine, the recipes, the early mover advantage, the location, and the reviews, we will never fully capture the shared memories, the word of mouth, and the reasons why Karim's has made it to every friend and food expert's list of recommendations in Delhi. But we try.

Speaking of Delhi's old-timer stories, I spoke with Anubhav Sapra, the founder of Delhi Food Walks, about the legendary status of the Karim's brand. In his experience, most tourists already know of Karim's when they travel to the city. On Anubhav's tours, it is always Karim's nihari for breakfast and their mutton seekh kabab and qorma in the evenings. For the adventurous, he recommends the brain curry. For Anubhav, what is special about their nihari is it is made of mutton and not beef. The ambience, the theatrical experience, and the assurance of hygiene are additional factors that make Karim's a must on Delhi Food Walk's list.

The last person Anubhav took to Karim's as a part of his tour was Dan Toombs, also known as The Curry Guy. He is the author of eight curry cookbooks so far, his ninth being a work in progress. Dan could not have been more excited about his experience at Karim's: 'It was a real treat to visit Karim's with Anubhav! Of the several places we went to, Karim's was one of the highlights. It is no wonder the restaurant has been open since 1913. The food there was out of this world! We had the nargisi kofta and mutton qorma. Both were incredible. I cannot wait to go back.'

The Journey Continues

Over the last century, Karim's has not just sustained but has grown manifold. Their legacy and the legendary status are now set in stone. The food is safe, wrapped in layers of secrecy. The cuisine continues to gain more and more followers as what constitutes Mughlai fare is understood better and more widely.

The family is happy with the expansion, though it was a difficult decision in the beginning. They believe that the changing climate, water, and air all affect the taste of the food. But it is a necessity for the growing family. The focus seems to be on keeping the food as close to the original while spreading their branches. This is why Karim's is the epic tale of evolving to stay the same.

The family remembers how in the early twentieth century, people did not eat out in restaurants much. But gradually, teachers, government employees, and private professionals began to visit. They used to pay a monthly sum in advance and ate regularly. From that era to now, the owners of Karim's are happy to have fed multiple generations of the same families. Seeing the growing number of teenagers in the restaurant lately has made them immensely satisfied, a signifier that the brand continues to resonate with newer generations.

But not all change is acceptable to the family. A burger chain wanted to package their qorma gravy as a sauce. Someone else came up with an idea for a pizza with their meat toppings. They have said no to all such offers. As food writer Damini Ralleigh describes, Karim's is 'an enduring legacy'. Whether through partnership, franchise, or by infringing on copyright, many desire to partake in that legacy.

In 2022, Karim's reached the Delhi High Court with a trademark infringement suit against Kareem Dhanani who ran Kareem's. Having started in 2003, Kareem's already had forty-one restaurants around the world. Karim's initiated action against Kareem Dhanani in 2015 with a legal notice and a case at the Intellectual Property Appellate Board. Relief came in 2022 when the court ordered Kareem's not to open any further restaurants under the name; and to issue public notices and add a disclaimer in their advertisements stating 'No connection with Karim's Jama Masjid/Delhi'.

Today, Karim's is a brand that has a seat amongst the legends. There may be many imitations of it in times to come. However, the biggest challenge to keeping the brand experience intact will probably be from the franchises and its expanding footprint. For the time being, there is no cause for concern. The tables are always occupied, the kabab sigri is smouldering, and the queues outside only keep getting longer.

Must-have Dishes at Karim's

Firdausi qorma

The menu describes it as a rare Mughlai mutton recipe. In comparison with Jahangiri which is a spicier gravy, this is a milder version with a delicious caramel-coloured gravy that both complements and highlights the taste of the meat. The soft khameeri rotis are the perfect accompaniment to scoop up the gravy.

Nargisi kofta

This has to be one of the best egg dishes ever created. A boiled egg is wrapped in a layer of exquisite minced meat and then fried. The meat is spiced to balance the egg, and it is then cooked in a qorma-like rich gravy. This must be tried because no egg has ever been treated this royally.

Mutton burrah

If you have tried burrahs before, you know the dish sounds simple, but very few get it right. Karim's is one of those few. The spicing of these large chunks of grilled mutton has never missed the mark, and the char on the bone is perfect as is the cook on the meat. The best thing about the dish is that the cuts always have enough meat on the bone.

Tandoori fish

This is a winter specialty and worth the wait. It is a whole fish that is spiced and roasted in the tandoor. While the skin is nicely charred, the meat inside is cooked just right. It is highly recommended because very few do it at all and no one so well.

Baqarkhani kulcha

Also known as sheermal, this is a baked sweet bread made with white flour and butter. It is mildly sweet, with shallow perforations to keep it from puffing. You may pair it with a spicy gravy or enjoy the bread by itself. It is impossible to appreciate its brilliance until eaten.

LOOKING TO THE FUTURE, STAYING TRUE TO THE PAST

Ram Ashraya, Mumbai (112)

Aatish Nath

At Mumbai's Ram Ashraya, the epitome of an Udupi restaurant, there's a precision to the way dishes reach your table and to how they are cleared once you have wiped the plates clean. First, a stainless steel tumbler of water is put down within minutes of you being directed to your seat at a table. Next, for those who are new, you consult the menu that is handwritten on a black stone wall or chat with your server for recommendations. The handwritten method of displaying the menu hasn't changed since the eatery first opened in Matunga in 1939. Back then, and even now, the dishes on the menu include South Indian specialities like upma, butter idlis, Mysore masala dosa, and filter coffee, among others. As a result, the restaurant is an anchor in a city that is constantly remaking itself.

A meal at Ram Ashraya is a chance to catch a breath, as the staff and the city swirls around you. Loyalists are happy to wait despite an almost perpetual queue. They could choose to head to the multitude of options within a five-minute walk, some with almost identical menus, but they don't mind sweating it out. The reward? Dosas that are layered in a thin film of ghee that doesn't wash off your hands. The fluffiest idlis that have an added bite from the whole fenugreek seeds in the chutney that you dip them into. Pineapple sheera, a halwa made of semolina, studded with raisins and pineapple pieces.

Over the decades, the eatery has not changed its interiors or its way of functioning. However, their daily standard operating procedures could be the inspiration for social media friendly restaurant design. The names of dishes get wiped off when the kitchen runs out of them. The seating is a mix of plastic chairs and two-seater benches that face easy-to-clean light wood veneered tables. The staff are friendly and warm, always prioritizing efficiency. And yet, what sets it apart is the weathering over the years—not distressed, but instead lived-in imperfections that come from decades of use.

There is peeling paint and cracks on almost every wall of the eatery. The printed photos of Lord Krishna, Ganesha, and Balaji displayed seemingly at random across the restaurant's walls have faded in their frames. Each frame has a built-in shelf for a frequent offering of flowers that dry out over the course of the day, and Tulsi leaves that are replaced three times a week. The floor tiles too are chipped in places. In a nod to the times, the bills are electronic instead of handwritten, and a square digital payments speaker sits on the counter for those who want to pay via their phones. Otherwise, regulars will find that not much else has changed, and that is what has made the restaurant a beloved icon in an area filled with legendary eateries.

Catering to a New Suburb

It was in the 1930s that Matunga first saw the establishment of Udupi restaurants around King's Circle, many of them surviving to this day. The locality was created by the British who bought the farmland and paddy fields here and converted them into the suburb that has grown to what we see today. The circle was the centrepiece of the area's development. The locality stood apart for its planned inclusion of open spaces, given that the entire neighbourhood was laid out to relieve congestion in the aftermath of the bubonic plague that struck the city in 1896.

Unsurprisingly, it was also where commerce thrived soon after. In 1935, a tram service connected Matunga and Dadar, around 3 kilometres apart, to the areas of Fort and Colaba (a distance of around 16 kilometres). This route linked the commercial heart of the city, extending up to King's Circle. Even after the tram service stopped in 1964, it remains one of the most well-connected districts by public transport.

Ram Ashraya was founded by Shyambabu Shetty in 1939 with humble goals—to provide a source of income for his family. At the age of thirty-nine, he had come to what was then called Bombay, alone, as a migrant from Kaup (pronounced Ka-Pu) in Karnataka and started what would become the iconic Ram Ashraya as a simple four-seater restaurant.

Ram Ashraya is closer to the Matunga Railway Station and is within walking distance of King's Circle and the King's Circle Railway Station. It is located on the corner of Bhandarkar Road, which connects to the arterial Eastern

Express Highway (once known as Kingsway) at one end and Lakhamsi Napoo Road at the other. In 1923, the Victoria Jubilee Technical Institute (now named Veermata Jijabai Technological Institute) moved from Byculla to its new home in Matunga, heralding the inhabitation of the suburb.

The impetus, says Amarjeeth Shetty, the third generation to now run this Udupi restaurant way before the term was attributed to such places, was to offer authentic South Indian food at affordable prices. Amarjeeth grandfather's brother would tell him of the time when tea cost 3 paisa, coffee was 5 paisa, idli would set one back 15 paisa, and a dosa was 25 paisa.

Shyambabu had a captive target group given that Matunga was a newly minted suburb, filling with South Indian migrants right from the 1930s onwards. Amarjeeth, who has been running the business for fourteen years, says with this influx from South India, as many as nineteen restaurants, both big and small, popped up to cater to the demand for the region's cuisine.

Eighty Years and Going Strong

Over the years, Ram Ashraya expanded and now occupies a corner of the ground floor of Jamnadas Mansion, a horseshoe-shaped building on Bhandarkar Road. It has taken over four of the ground floor shops in the building and sits between Quality Tea & Coffee shop and Laxmi Jewellery Mart. Its expansion though began only in the 1960s when Shyambabu's sons, Jayaram and Bhaskar Shetty, joined the restaurant. They set it up as we know it today, with seventy-two seats, the wooden register at the entrance, and the mithai area.

In 1999, the third generation was inducted into the business with Akshay, the eldest of Jayaram's sons, joining the business. Soon, Amarjeeth, Jayaram's younger son, also came on board and together, they saw themselves as stewards of their family's vision. Amarjeeth's father and uncle chose not to expand to different locations the way another entrepreneur Rama Nayak was doing at the time (he opened his first outlet in 1938). Instead, they chose to maintain the quality and service that their diners were accustomed to, while expanding the existing restaurant and taking over a corner of the street. 'It is not the number of restaurants that define you, but rather holding the one place you have close to your heart and doing it full justice,' explains Amarjeeth.

Since joining the business at the age of twenty-four, Amarjeeth has immersed himself in its day-to-day operations. He did, however, venture out on his own, working and pursuing other passions before coming back to Ram Ashraya. 'Joining the family business was more of a responsibility...' Amarjeeth says, and he trails off, seeming more than content with his decision. He explains how he and Akshay, who is five years older, complement each other, 'Whatever I miss, he points out to me, and vice versa. And we encourage each other so that the business blooms.'

Amarjeeth has been deeply engaged in the restaurant and its functioning over the years. He can reel off everything, from the ingredients in a batter to the price of dishes. He knows the names of all of the approximately sixty-five employees who work for him and spends some part of each day at the restaurant office, located one floor above the eatery. The large wooden desk is imposing, but it's the images of three gods that immediately catch the eye. To the right of his desk, large frames house images of Goddess Lakshmi, Lord Krishna astride Garuda, and the Virat Swaroop of Lord Vishnu.

From Kaup to Matunga

The black handwritten menu at Ram Ashraya boasts mostly food from Kaup, the Shetty's hometown. Amarjeeth reels off items like buns puri, goli bajji, kela bajji, and dal vada—items he says are a 'part of Udupi culture'. While most visitors stop by for idlis, their dosas, vadas, and the buns puri (or Mangalore buns as they are also called) remain popular. It comprises two fist-sized puris served with chutney and sambar. The batter for this is fermented overnight and is made of mashed bananas, flour, yoghurt, sugar, and salt. It has a doughy consistency and is then individually portioned and fried. The goli bajji, on the other hand, are lemon-sized balls with a crispy fried exterior and chewy inside. It is a very satisfying snack.

During the festive season, which is after Onam and the city's ten-day-long Ganpati celebration, the restaurant sees a surge of visitors, usually South Indians, who have come to the area. 'They have this soft corner for a place where they know they will get buns puri, goli bajji, and kela bajji. There was a time when these items could be had anywhere, but now, all these traditional dishes are hard to find and are available only at a select few places,' explains Amarjeeth. He's aware that the restaurant is both a place to relive nostalgia and a keeper of an identity, tied to his own culture and the way in which he grew up.

Over the years, though, as tastes have evolved, Ram Ashraya has tweaked the menu, taking feedback from their diners into account. Amarjeeth wants to believe these recipes belong to their customers: 'Right from the time of our predecessors, whatever the customer demanded we gave it a proper hearing and tried to inculcate it in our taste. This has been a continuous thing where whatever the customer demands, we try and provide it.'

For example, Amarjeeth points to the fact that customers at the eatery can order a single idli or single medu vada, something that isn't normally offered at other similar restaurants in the city. 'In the scheme of doing business, the restaurant tends to lose money this way because the ticket size becomes smaller,' he explains. While it's not that Ram Ashraya incurs loss on a single item order, the profits are lower for the restaurant on a per plate basis. However, Amarjeeth sees this as a luxury—giving the customer the option of a single item from a two-piece order.

Opposite the register sit two vitrines filled with Indian sweets. Inside you'll see sweets which, unlike the dining menu, span the breadth of the country—from gulab jamun to malai sandwich, kesar peda to rava ladoo. Each mithai is sold in individual portions or in small plastic takeaway containers. Choose from the ghee and gram flour-based Mysore Pak or the ever-popular badam halwa. For festivities and celebrations at home, it is the quarter kilo and half kilo boxes that are popular. The mithai section at Ram Ashraya was there from the start, though it was discontinued briefly for a few years in between. The expansion of its offerings to a pan-Indian selection happened about five to seven years ago.

Moulded by the City

Matunga has always been considered a South Indian enclave. The area, though, has also always been home to other communities. As Vikram Doctor, a journalist who writes about food and its role in India explains, 'One thumb rule about Bombay is that any food trend that is mostly vegetarian, you tend to find Gujaratis behind it.' In Matunga it was no different, with Ram Ashraya attracting traders, clerks, and families from across community lines—including Gujaratis, the all-encompassing South Indians, Parsis, and Hindus. As part of the original blueprint, Matunga–Dadar had residential enclaves for both Parsi and Hindu communities, with each providing housing to 200–300 families.

In much of the city, the Udupi restaurants have changed with the times, taking both commercial considerations and audience preferences into account. Ram Ashraya has remained true to its roots, eschewing adding an air-conditioned section or upgrading the menu to include North Indian or Chindian fare. However, when it comes to its recipes, many have suggested that the restaurants in the area, Ram Ashraya included, have sweetened their sambar over time to appeal to Gujarati tastes. But this is something that Amarjeeth pushes back on, 'Our style of sambar does not lean towards Gujarati or Jain, it's more the Udupi Brahmin style cooking. So people have this preconceived notion ke agar kanda lasan nahi dalte toh (if onion and garlic are not added), we are trying to appease Gujaratis and Jains.' For Amarjeeth, his family has grown up with these recipes, and so there aren't any significant changes made to appeal to any specific community.

'If we were to compromise on the taste, we wouldn't

have this kind of footfall from all kinds of people, irrespective of gender, race, or caste,' Amarjeeth points out, adding that this taste is the foundation on which they built the brand that they are today. Whatever the caste and purity implications, Ram Ashraya is also an institution because it cuts across social classes. As long as someone can afford a meal there, they're welcome. Prices are pretty reasonable, though possibly a meal for two might no longer be affordable to a blue-collar worker. Today, a cup of tea is still only ₹26, an idli plate costs ₹57, and a masala dosa is ₹75. Compare that to McDonalds, where the cheapest burger in 2023 is more than ₹100. No wonder the restaurant goes through 1,000 litres of sambar, 200 kilograms of idli batter, and 250 kilograms of dosa batter daily.

To ensure that dishes reach customers as soon as possible, a team of about thirty-five men, working in two shifts, toil away in the kitchen. Divided into two distinct rooms, the kitchen includes four people washing dishes and two others overseeing the wet grinders which run from morning to closing to make batter that is either serving immediate needs or being prepared for the next day. The rest can be found at various stations, making dosas, steaming idlis, and pouring sambar and chutney into individual containers. Vinod Yadav started as a dishwasher in the kitchen in 2001, when he moved to the city from Jharkhand. Devoid of any connections in the metropolis, he found a job with Ram Ashraya, and over the years has moved up to the post of head of operations. Now, he oversees the weekly delivery of ingredients and works in the kitchen every day.

The restaurant employs twenty-five waiters, who also work in two shifts, starting at 3.30 a.m. to cater to customers that start streaming in from 5 a.m. The restaurant closes at 9 p.m. The men can be seen ferrying egg yolk yellow trays from the metal pass, where ready orders sit in the liminal space between being made and being served to the many tables. Most servers are dressed in a white shirt and black pants. After a final clean-up and ensuring that the batters are made for the next day, and if necessary, fermenting, the staff leave at 10 p.m.

One distinctive aspect is their bare feet. Amarjeeth doesn't even remember how it started, 'but they don't wear footwear when they are on the floor. It's kind of a dedication to the service they are providing.'

People's Choice

Shikha Bafna, a gemologist in Italy, had lived in Mumbai for four years during which visits to Ram Ashraya became a regular ritual. What set it apart for her was 'the simplicity of the place and how ordinary it was; it didn't ask too much of you, you can just show up, eat, and leave'. That ordinariness is what gives it universal appeal—

transcending classes and social hierarchy to remain a great leveller in a city where everyone is constantly striving upwards.

Every diner has their reason for making their way to Ram Ashraya. For a couple from the Czech Republic visiting on one September afternoon, it was due to a recommendation by an Indian friend who lives there. For a lone policewoman, her badge and uniform covered with a jacket, it was to enjoy a plate of idli and sambar as a quick and nourishing break. For two college students, it was the cooling effect of the nimbu pani paired with a dosa each. For a mother–daughter duo from Cuffe Parade, it was the proximity of the restaurant after work that got them to the area one evening.

Each found their way there, for the first time in their lives or the first time that particular week for a quick pit stop. Weekend mornings see eager customers lining up outside the restaurant. Sometimes the line sees a wait of an hour or more and Amarjeeth suggests avoiding visiting the restaurant between 7 a.m. and 10 a.m. and during the evening snack time when there's usually a queue.

When it comes to filter coffee, they serve as many as 1,000 cups a day. Regulars swear by its invigorating properties and a taste that tips pleasingly towards bitterness. Priced at ₹32, it seems like a steaming cup can be found on every table. For Dr Aditya Deshmukh, who was a house doctor in the psychiatry department at Sion Hospital and is currently studying for his post-graduate degree, 'the filter coffee is what sets Ram Ashraya apart', and he calls it 'a complete standout'. He has been getting his regular caffeine fix here since moving to the city seven years ago.

Amarjeeth is circumspect about the popularity that the restaurant and certain dishes now enjoy. 'I must say, there's always ups and downs in the business. This level of popularity wasn't there always,' he notices. He has seen a lot and observes that every decade or so, there's a slowdown that can be attributed to economic trends. Though every morning at 5 a.m., when he opens the shop, it's the motley group of customers waiting that makes him realize the restaurant's reach. Many times, the party-hard twenty-somethings stop by for a quick breakfast at the break of dawn, from a limited menu that features tea, coffee, idlis, vada, rasam, upma, and sheera, before heading home to finally sleep the night off. Then there are fitness enthusiasts and daily labourers. Recently, it's morning cycling groups that make a pit stop at the restaurant for breakfast and a coffee. From 7 a. m. onwards, the entire menu is available to order.

Abhishek Shetty, the second-generation co-owner of Sadanand Hotel, another Udupi restaurant in Mumbai's Crawford Market, an older area of the city closer to Fort explains what keeps these restaurants running over multiple generations: 'The price point has been the most important, with meals available to all, especially single men who need daily sustenance as they went about work in the city. Today a masala dosa at Sadanand costs ₹130. Cleanliness is the second. Everyone knows that an Udupi restaurant is where diners can look in and see their food being prepared and coming to them. We are proud of showing off our space.' Finally, he points to the dishes on offer and explains, 'It is comfort food. They know what the food is—they know it's idli, vada, and dosa. It's been there for generations; they've been eating it as kids and they just keep coming back in, thanks to the price factor.' In Matunga, Ram Ashraya catered to both single men who lived in tenements and families that had moved to the suburbs in search of space and cheaper rents.

Just like with the city's local trains, which require careful planning to squeeze into or out of during peak hours, it may feel the same at Ram Ashraya for a regular visitor. But it is rewarding once they've found the dishes they want to return for and know the best times to avoid the wait. Acknowledging this, Amarjeeth agrees that it works in the restaurant's favour to have age-old customers who know exactly what they want to have.

In practice though, that's not the case, with the restaurant constantly attracting new diners. Amarjeeth is aware of the needs of a first-time visitor and explains how the restaurant's waiters serve as a bridge. 'We have a limited menu, and we make it to the best of our ability. Even when a new diner comes in and they don't know what to have, the waiters have a one-on-one interaction with the customers they serve and guide them. Otherwise, it would just be transactional—we give you food and you give us money and nothing more, nothing less—which is not what Ram Ashraya has made its name for over multiple generations,' he elaborates. For Amarjeeth, three things are ingrained in his staff: it's all about the quality; it's all about the service; it's all about the cleanliness.

Matunga resident Sachin Gandhi has been going to Ram Ashraya for over twenty-five years and says that he prefers some of the dishes that they do over other restaurants in the area—specifically the dosa, the Mysore dosa, and idlis. But he finds the 'new' post-Covid sambar spicier and less sour.

Like him, people here can be picky because those craving South Indian—the catch-all term for idlis and dosas—are spoiled for choice in Matunga. Speak to anyone who's grown up in and around the area and they'll have their favourite spot—whether it be Cafe Madras, Mysore Cafe, or A. Rama Nayak & Sons Udupi, all of which are also institutions. Most have sampled the food at some of these restaurants and then weighed their choices to make a decision.

As the third-generation owner, Amarjeeth when he first took over saw his role as one of slowly improving the restaurant's back-end operations. He noticed that 'tweaking was needed to sharpen processes, to procure the best material at an affordable price, and to get things in order'. Most of the restaurant's suppliers have been with them since his father's time. Amarjeeth has utmost faith in them and is of the firm belief that a business like his is only as good as the vendors he has. 'People tell us that they came forty years ago and even today the taste remains the same,' he concludes.

For Dr Aditya, it hasn't been forty years, but he remembers coming for the first time as a twelve-year-old with his father when he was visiting the city from Nanded. Now he practises at Sion Hospital and makes his way to the restaurant quite often, but he knows to avoid the weekend crowds. Instead, Dr Aditya visits on Monday mornings to start the week off on the right note. Marvelling at their quality control, he says, 'I still remember my dad talking about it because he has been going to Ram Ashraya for the last thirty years or so, and he still says their taste has not changed a bit.'

Given the choices that have exploded for diners in the years since the country's economic liberalization in 1991, Amarjeeth is aware that Ram Ashraya is just one of many restaurants that diners can choose to go to. While that's always been the case in Matunga, where other restaurants have also survived through the years—the offerings have now expanded to include everything from waffles to frankies available within a ten-minute walk of the restaurant. As Amarjeeth explains, 'It's not about the amount of money, but diners are smart enough about where they want to put their money. They want taste they can relate to.'

Future Gazing

Amidst construction of a city-wide underground metro line and Mumbai's Coastal Road project, it is no surprise that on a neighbourhood level, Matunga is also being rebuilt. The old buildings, some with balconies, others with distinctive wooden doors, are coming down to make way for towers that touch the sky. Ram Ashraya's current address, Jamnadas Mansion, has been purchased by a builder, and so it will be demolished in the near future.

Since January 2022 when it was bought for redevelopment, the Shetty family has been in search of a new location for the iconic eatery. Like with so much else with the business, the Shetty brothers left it up to the divine. Amarjeeth says, 'We used to just pray to God to show us whatever is suitable and left it up to him.'

Their prayers were answered. Exactly two weeks after their building was purchased, a property opposite the restaurant, which housed a bank for six or seven years, vacated. Through what the Shettys believe is divine intervention, they got it. According to Amarjeeth, 'Our main motive was our customers should not lose out just because we have shifted to someplace else or we couldn't find a place.'

Since August 2022, there have been two outlets of Ram Ashraya within metres of each other, with the newer outlet having replaced the branch of Bharat Cooperative Bank on Laxmi Narayan Lane. At some point, the original outlet will be shuttered and, it is assumed, reopened in the future at the base of a swanky new building.

With its closure, the restaurant's patrons will have to start a new morning routine, past the kabootar khana (pigeon house) built on a triangular plot opposite the original restaurant, towards another corner spot where a bigger ninety-seat eatery awaits. There the menu can be found pasted on the walls, instead of being handwritten, but it still retains the exceptionally quick service and local favourites. What has changed is the inclusion of other styles of idlis—like the larger Kanchipuram and thatte idlis alongside the button idlis. Each of these idlis requires a different batter, and while the Kanchipuram idli is steamed in the mantharai (*Bauhinia variegata* or the orchid tree) the thatte idli batter includes both rice and urad dal.

There are also set South Indian meals on the menu now. With the set meals, Amarjeeth aims to recreate the time of vegetarian lunch homes that were aplenty in the area. 'Now all over Mumbai, you will find a handful of these players who serve authentic South Indian thalis. As an old institution, we thought of expanding our menu instead of having the same dishes.' The hearty meal includes chapatis, one dry vegetable, one that's in a gravy, rasam, sambar, dal, rice, curd, pickle, papad, chili, and payasam.

On Currey Road, Ram Ashraya has another outlet that was opened in February 2022. The reason, Amarjeeth elaborates, was the pandemic. After it subsided, they thought they should reach out to more people, with a lot of them being vegetarians based in South Mumbai. A large number of their clientele comes from town side, from Kalbadevi and Marine Drive. As a result, the brand has been keen to get closer to that section of diners, especially with the way the city is expanding. Right now, Amarjeeth sees Lalbaug as the beginning of town. The new outlet is air-conditioned, a first for the restaurant, and once again, the menu has been expanded to include pav bhaji, tawa pulao, and juices like sugarcane, watermelon, and pineapple.

Amarjeeth has learned the fact that change is the only constant. It's clear that Ram Ashraya is working to strike a balance between its storied history and keeping up with the times. The new Matunga location frees the family; they can now innovate, even as those walking in expect the same quality and taste that the restaurant is known for. As the space is unfettered by history, it allows for experimentation. The last time that something new was added to the menu in Matunga was 2008, when seasonal fruit sheeras were introduced. In the years since, the pineapple sheera has joined the list of dishes that the original location is now identified with, and as Amarjeeth notes, 'by God's grace we are synonymous with sheera'.

Speaking of the fourth generation that may be initiated into the business, Amarjeeth considers it their responsibility to think how the family can work on keeping the business simple while simultaneously growing it. That way it makes it easy for the next generation. He also wants his children to see that they're doing more than just running an enterprise. 'We're doing this not only for business, but more from the point of view of rendering a service,' he says. In an era where everyone and everything is a brand, Amarjeeth wants to prove to diners that 'it's not only about fame but the hard work behind that keeps the show running'.

Ultimately, everything that the present generation is doing is in service to a larger goal. Amarjeeth is clear that both he and his brother are merely stewards of a business that serves present needs while looking to the future: 'It was a vision given to us by our family. They told us "you can become legendary by focusing on one place", and that is a vision that we have carried forward.'

Today, Ram Ashraya is testimony to that vision—of preserving the past while looking towards the future. Changes are incremental unless forced by circumstance, but the commitment to certain tenets has stayed firm. It's why the eatery continues to have a loyal following across generations and geography, with visitors making it a point to stop for filter coffee and a snack at any time of the day. Over multiple visits, it becomes clear that the restaurant operates like a well-oiled machine, with staff members always in motion as they work to ensure that meals are ordered, eaten, and taken away as quickly as possible. However, I never felt hustled as I savoured a dosa or dug into the rasam vada. Instead, I felt a warmth that permeates the experience—knowing that mine was an experience craved by others. One that balances efficiency and nostalgia in equal measure.

Must-have Dishes at Ram Ashraya

Pineapple sheera

A much loved addition to the menu, the pineapple sheera is one of many flavours that were initially made available. Served in a metal katori, the rounded scoop is larger than a traditional ice cream serving and speckled with semolina. It's only when you bite into the pineapple pieces that that you understand how the puckering but sweet fruit holds its own and complements the cloyingly sweet dish. The two spoons it comes with (even for a sole diner's order) hints that it can be shared, but a portion is small enough that it could serve as a sweet snack or indulgent dessert for one. Ultimately, it is the raisin and pineapple aftertaste that lingers, giving this dish a unique complexity.

Rasam vada

The rasam at Ram Ashraya is not sinus-clearing or overly peppery. Instead, it's just the right amount of sour—the kind that might cause you to break into a sweat in Mumbai's humid heat. The spongy vadas are small enough that they have fully soaked through, which makes them easier to eat and more flavourful than some stodgier ones found in the city. Whether ordered as a snack or as an accompaniment to other dishes, the tangy rasam ensures it stands out on any table.

Filter coffee

The distinctive davara tumbler set that the filter coffee is served in can be spotted as soon as you enter Ram Ashraya. It may be on a table, in a customer's hands, being cooled table side by a waiter, or have left a coffee ring on a table that's waiting to be cleaned. The much-loved drink is served throughout the day. The source of the coffee beans is a well-guarded secret, but even over decades, it has managed to remain consistent. The sweetness seems perfectly calibrated to leave a faint bitter aftertaste.

Ghee podi idli

Idlis are a popular order, alongside the various kinds of dosas on offer. Served steaming, they are topped with a generous layer of dry podi, over which ghee is then spooned. There's a bite that remains from the crunchy podi, while also bursting with flavours—spicy and sour—all coming together on a hot, spongy idli.

Buns puri

For those that want to have something sweet, without it being cloying, consider the buns puri. A traditional Udupi family dish, the large fist-sized puris are crusty on the outside, suggesting a filling. However, once you tear into the pliant puri, it's the surprise of the crisp exterior giving way to a soft puri that underlines the complexity of this popular dish. Each bite has a hint of banana-led sweetness that is balanced with the sourness of the fermentation process. This is best paired with the coconut chutney that it is served with.

REFERENCES

LEGENDS ARE MADE OF THIS

vii **In June 2023, when Taste Atlas released its list:** Taste Atlas (@tasteatlas), Post, 23 June 2023, <www.instagram.com/p/Ct1xN9fI59W>.; Priya Raghuvanshi, 'Murthal's Amrik Sukhdev among 7 Indian eateries in World's Most Legendary Restaurants list; check out the names', *Business Today*, 26 June 2023.

vii **In December 2023, Taste Atlas released revised rankings:** '150 Most Legendary Restaurants in the World & Their Iconic Dishes', Taste Atlas, 12 December 2023, available at www.tasteatlas.com/iconic-dishes-legendary-restaurants.

A PARAGON OF CULINARY EXCELLENCE

3 **The story goes that a high-ranking British official:** Sumesh Govind in conversation with the author, 12 July 2023.

13 **Paragon uses what they refer to as leg-on chicken:** Ibid.

14 **Actress Sunny Leone visited the outlet.:** Paragon Restaurant Calicut, Post, 4 September 2023, <www.facebook.com/paragonrestaurantcalicut/videos/paragon-restaurant-calicut/626873996187028>.

14 **Emirati YouTuber, vlogger, and digital content creator**: 'I Flew 2000 Miles For Biryani', Post, 14 July 2023, <www.youtube.com/watch?v=_A2g0DJxva8>.

THE KABABS THAT HAVE DEFINED LUCKNOW FOR OVER A CENTURY

26 **The nawabs were connoisseurs of good food:** Mehru Jaffer in conversation with author, 11 September 2023.

26 **With time, Shuja-ud-Daula's son Asaf-ud-Daula.**: Ibid.

27 **According to word on the street, the unique dishes**: Ibid.

30 **Now on on to the story of the one-handed kababchi.**: Mohammad Usman in conversation with author, 1 September 2023.

31 **Rais Ahmad is said to have expanded the business:** Mohammad Usman in conversation with author, 1 September 2023.

31 **Commonly known as Mughlai paratha:** Taiyaba Ali in conversation with author, September 2023.

36 **Legend has it that the proprietary masala:** Professor Pushpesh Pant in conversation with author, September 2023.

40 **Most others who visit the restaurant:** this has been gleaned through many conversations the author has had with travellers during Lucknow with Anubhuti, an experiential food tour of the city that is hosted by her.

40 **one outlet sells over 100 kilograms of biryani:** Mohammad Usman in conversation with author, 1 September 2023.

NOSTALGIA AND THE MAKING OF A LEGEND

49 **In the second half of the nineteenth century:** Trinanjan Chakraborty, 'The Armenian Racing and Real-estate King of Colonial Calcutta', *The Telegraph*, 23 May 2023.; Viren Adolf D'Sa. 'The Armenian Orthodox Community of India – A tribute to a once highly influential community in a secular country!', *Bombay Experience*, 12 July 2015.

51 **The entrance to the restaurant is on Middleton Row:** 'About School', LoretoHouseKolkata.com, available at www.loretohousekolkata.com/aboutSchool.aspx.; Padmini Sathianadhan Sengupta, *A Hundred Years of Service: Centenary Volume of the Calcutta Y.W.C.A.*, 1878–1978, Kolkata: Bibhash Gupta for the Y.W.C.A. of Calcutta, p. 81.

51 **The lane where Peter Cat stands today:** Evan Cotton, *Calcutta Old and New: A Historical and Descriptive Handbook to the City*, Calcutta: W. Newman & Co., p. 286.; Kathleen Blechynden, *Calcutta: Past and Present*, Calcutta: W. Thacker & Co., 1905, p. 211.

52 **The land on which Stephen Court was built:** 'Stephen Court, the history and the height', *The Telegraph*, 25 March 2010.

53 **The Kotharis are originally from Kutch in Gujarat.:** Nitin Kothari in conversation with author, 17 August 3023.

55 **Historian Antonella Viola confirms this in her essay**: Antonella Viola, 'The Italian...who Comes Here to try his Luck... Only Deals in Trade: Italian Traders in Bengal 1850–1950 ca.', in *Bengal and Italy: Transcultural Encounters from the Mid-19th to the Early 21st Century*, Paromita Chakravarti and Mario Prayer (eds.), New York: Routledge, 2023, p. 167.

56 **In the late 60s, while the rest of Bengal and Calcutta:** Sumanta Banerjee, *In the Wake of Naxalbari*, Kolkata: Sahitya Samsad, p. 224.

58 **Najmieh Batmanglij, in the book**: Najmieh Batmanglij, *Food of Life: Ancient Persian and Modern Iranian Cooking and Ceremonies*, Washington DC: Mage Publishers, 2020, p. 120.

61 **One X (formerly Twitter) user even tweeted:** Anindya (@anindya0909), Post, X.com, 1 December 2022, < https://twitter.com/anindya0909/status/1598329610139467777>.

61 **The second most ordered dish at Peter Cat:** this insight has been gleaned by the author from her conversations with Nitin Kothari and regulars at the restaurant.

THE DHABA THAT BIRTHED A TOWN

74 **Amrik Singh's uncle, Sardar Lakshman Singh:** Amrik Singh and Suraj Singh in conversation with the author, 22 September 2023.

77 **India was hosting the ninth Asian Games.:** '1982 Asian Games: Know all about when India last hosted the Asiad', *Hindustan Times*, 22 September 2023.

81 **A large number of people from the state of Punjab:** Manjeet Sehgal, 'Why Punjab is seeing reverse migration amid sweeping external exodus', *India Today*, 17 May 2023.

82 **Sonipat Municipal Corporation served demolition notices:** Manvir Saini, 'Murthal Dhabas face threat of demolition', *Times of India*, 16 January 2018.

A FAMILY'S COMMITMENT TO CONSISTENCY

103 **Next up was the rava idli, a MTR creation:** Hemamalini Maiya in conversation with the author, 6 September 2023.

105 **In 1976, during the Emergency:** Hemamalini Maiya, *The Coffee Story*, press note, 6 September 2023.

A CUISINE, A CENTURY, A LEGEND

121 **The name came about in part thanks to another family**: Haji Karimuddin's family in conversation with the author, 23 August 2023.

126 **India's grain production crashed to one-fifth**: S. A. Aiyar, 'Drought not a big calamity in India anymore', *Times of India*, 29 July 2012.

126 **As royalty became history, the customers of Mughlai:** Haji Karimuddin's family in conversation with the author.

126 **According to Salma Hussain, a historian:** Anand Raj OK, 'A history of Mughal cuisine: Salma Husain reveals culinary secrets of the royal kitchens', *Friday*, 25 January 2021.

128 **Eating Out in Delhi, a now defunct food group:** Hemanshu Kumar, 'Karim's', *Eating Out in Delhi*, 21 November 2008.

131 **Cynthia Rosenfeld wrote in her review:** Cynthia Rosenfield, 'Restaurant Review: Karim Hotel, New Delhi, India', *New York Times*, 27 March 2009.

131 **that traces its roots to the kitchens of emperor:** Haji Karimuddin's family in conversation with the author.

131 **'Karim's had transformed from a local purveyor':** Alex Traub and Zehra Kazmi, 'Haji Zahooruddin, who upheld the traditions of Karim's, dies at 85', *Hindustan Times*, 1 February 2018.

135 **As food writer Damini Ralleigh describes:** Damini Ralleigh, 'An Enduring Legacy: The oldest member of Karim's, Zahooruddin, died at 85, leaving behind a living heritage', *Indian Express*, 6 February 2018.

135 **In 2022, Karim's reached the Delhi High Court:** Sounak Mukhopadhyay, 'Karim's or Kareem's: HC intervenes in tussle over brand name', *Mint Lounge*, 31 May 2022.; S. S. Rana &Co., 'The Mughal(ai) Battles of Modern India; Karim v/s Kareem', *Lexology*, 30 August 2022.

LOOKING TO THE FUTURE, STAYING TRUE TO THE PAST

142 **The locality was created by the British:** Nikhil Rao, *House, But No Garden: Apartment Living in Bombay Suburbs, 1898–1964*, Ann Arbor: University of Minnesota Press, p. 49.

142 **In 1935, a tram service connected Matunga and Dadar:** Ibid., p. 77.

143 **In 1923, the Victoria Jubilee Technical Institute:** 'History', Vjti.ac.in, available at vjti.ac.in/history.

148 **As part of the original blueprint, Matunga–Dadar:** Rao, *House, But No Garden*, p. 75.; Skye A. Thomas, 'Dadar Parsi Colony: A Deco of Plans', *Mumbai Mirror*, 27 November 2017.

148 **However, when it comes to its recipes:** Vikram Doctor in conversation with the author, 16 September 2023.

158 **A large number of their clientele comes from town side:** Amarjeeth Shetty in conversation with the author, 5 September 2023.

PICTURE CREDITS

Paragon Ventures Pvt Ltd.: **p. 1.**
Aakanksha Arun: **p. 23.**
Priyadarshini Chatterjee: **p. 47.**
Wikimedia Commons: **pp. 71, 93.**
Om Routray: **p. 117.**
Aatish Nath: **p. 139.**

NOTES ON THE CONTRIBUTORS

Ruth Dsouza Prabhu is an independent journalist based in Bengaluru, India, with over two decades of experience across media platforms. She has been published in leading national and international publications such as the *New York Times*, *Al Jazeera*, *The National*, *Whetstone SA*, *Fodor's Travel*, *Nikkei Asia*, *Eaten*, and *Good Beer Hunting* and has bylines in *Mint Lounge*, *Condé Nast Traveller*, *Architectural Digest*, *Travel + Leisure*, *Nat Geo Traveller*, *The Federal*, *Goya Journal*, *Paper Planes*, *Reader's Digest*, *Lifestyle Asia*, *The Hindu*, *Firstpost*, and *Zeezest*. She has written extensively for the now-defunct *Huffington Post India* and Smartlife from *The Week*. She has interviewed several celebrated chefs, including Marco Pierre White, Gaggan Anand, Garima Arora, and the MasterChef Australia trio—Gary Mehigan, Matt Preston, and George Calombaris. She has been on the jury panels for prestigious F&B Awards such as the Epicurean Guild Awards, Condé Nast Restaurant Awards, BW Hotelier Awards, and The Week Restaurant Awards.

Anubhuti Krishna is a writer and consultant based in New Delhi. Her work has featured extensively in major Indian dailies such as *The Hindu, Times of India, Mint Lounge, and Hindustan Times* and international travel and food magazines like *Condé Nast Traveller, Travel + Leisure, Goya Journal, Paper Planes,* and *Architectural Digest*. Her writing explores the complexities of India's diverse cuisines, vernacular architecture, and hyper local arts, crafts, and cultural practices. As someone who grew up around food and in a city like Lucknow, writing the essay on Tunday Kababi was a natural extension of her work—and life—in Lucknow where she regularly hosts Lucknow with Anubhuti, a two-day food and culture experience for travellers who hope to understand the city's nuanced culture and food. Tunday Kababi, naturally, features prominently on the itinerary. She is currently working on a full-fledged book on Lucknow and its food culture.

Priyadarshini Chatterjee is a food, culture, and travel writer based in Kolkata, India. Her work has appeared in a number of national and international publications including *BBC, Condé Nast Traveller India, Eater, Hindu Business Line, Lonely Planet India, Mint Lounge, Open Magazine, Scroll.in,* and *Whetstone Magazine*. She has dabbled in different genres of food writing—from blogging about family recipes to critiquing restaurants—before focusing her expertise on the intersections of food, history, and culture. She is particularly interested in exploring food in its historical contexts. When she isn't writing or researching about food, she can be found cooking up a storm in her kitchen.

Om Routray writes about food, society, and politics for various publications. He, along with his wife, runs ForkTales, a food experience and research initiative. He has worked in the agri-tech sector and has contributed extensively to agri-food policy, sustainability, and farmer welfare issues. He has featured on ET Now's Leaders of Tomorrow.

Aatish Nath is a freelance writer based in Mumbai. Having gotten his start at *Time Out Mumbai* as the magazine's food and drink editor, he has since covered the restaurant industry in the city for a host of news outlets. Over time, he has expanded to write about music, culture, and travel as well. His writing has appeared in *The Hindu*, *Travel + Leisure India*, *Citylab*, *National Geographic Traveller India*, *Brown Paper Bag*, *Firstpost*, *Condé Nast Traveller India*, *Vogue*, and *Soho House Notes*. His other interests include photography and cooking.

5-24